A Socratic Introduction to Plato's *Republic*

Other Works of Interest from St. Augustine's Press

Rémi Brague, *On the God of the Christians (& on one or two others)*

Rémi Brague, *Eccentric Culture: A Theory of Western Civilization*

Albert Camus, *Christian Metaphysics and Neoplatonism*

Edward Feser, *The Last Superstition: A Refutation of the New Atheism*

H.S. Gerdil, *The Anti-Emile: Reflections on the Theory and Practice of Education against the Principles of Rousseau*

Gerhard Niemeyer, *The Loss and Recovery of Truth*

James V. Schall, *The Regensburg Lecture*

James V. Schall, *The Modern Age*

Pierre Manent, *Seeing Things Politically*

Marc D. Guerra, *Liberating Logos: Pope Benedict XVI's September Speeches*

Peter Kreeft, *Ecumenical Jihad*

Peter Kreeft, *If Einstein Had Been a Surfer*

Peter Kreeft, *I Surf, Therefore I Am*

Peter Kreeft, *Jesus-Shock*

Peter Kreeft, *An Ocean Full of Angels*

Peter Kreeft, *The Philosophy of Jesus*

Peter Kreeft, *The Platonic Tradition*

Peter Kreeft, *The Sea Within*

Peter Kreeft, *Socratic Logic (3rd Edition)*

Peter Kreeft, *Summa Philosophica*

Ellis Sandoz, *Give Me Liberty: Studies on Constitutionalism and Philosophy*

Roger Kimball, *The Fortunes of Permanence: Culture and Anarchy in an Age of Amnesia*

A Socratic Introduction to Plato's *Republic*

Peter Kreeft

St. Augustine's Press
South Bend, Indiana

Manufactured in the United States of America.

1 2 3 4 5 6 24 23 22 21 20 19 18

Library of Congress Cataloging in Publication Data
Names: Kreeft, Peter, author.
Title: A Socratic introduction to Plato's Republic / Peter Kreeft.
Description: 1st [edition].
South Bend, Indiana: St. Augustine's Press, Inc, 2016.
Includes index.
Identifiers: LCCN 2016033720
ISBN 9781587318283 (hardcover: alk. paper)
Subjects: LCSH: Plato. Republic.
Socrates.
Philosophy--History.
Classification: LCC JC71.P6 K68 2016
DDC 321/.07--dc23 LC record available at
https://lccn.loc.gov/2016033720

¥ The paper used in this publication meets the minimum requirements of the American National Standard for Information Sciences - Permanence of Paper for Printed Materials, ANSI Z39.48-1984.

St. Augustine's Press
www.staugustine.net

For William Harry Jellema,
the how—almost—legendary matchmaker-philosopher
who put me on one end of the log and Plato on the other.
Much of this book is taken from his classes of Calvin College.

He spread the good infection to me
that I spread to you.

Contents

I. Introduction

1. Who is this book for?

This book is designed for three classes of people:

(1) Beginners who want an introduction to philosophy
(2) Those who have already had an introduction to philosophy and who would like to see it in action now applied to a great book written by a great philosopher, but who have never read Plato's *Republic*, the most famous and influential philosophy book ever written
(3) Those who have read Plato's *Republic* before but did not understand its deepest significance

All three of these classes of people can be found both inside the classrooms of formal education and outside classrooms, as do-it-yourselfers. They can also be found on various levels of formal education, and this book is designed for all of them:

(1) It is mainly designed for college students.
(2) It is also usable by bright high school students,
(3) and for curious do-it-yourselfers of all ages, whether they went to college or not.
(4) It is also usable by graduate students, either in philosophy or in some related field, who need a basic beginners' introduction to the *Republic*.
(5) It is not, however, designed for graduate or post-graduate scholarly research. It is only an *introduction*.

2. Why do you need philosophy?

Because you do not have a choice between having a philosophy and not having a philosophy. You only have a choice between having a good philosophy and having a bad one; between having one that you are aware of and think about, and having one without knowing you have it and without thinking about it. Hitler had a philosophy. So did Mother Teresa. It makes a great difference what kind of philosophy you have. Yet we're usually more picky about our pensions, our pleasures, and our pockets than our philosophies.

"Philosophy" means literally "the love of wisdom." What does this mean?

It means what it says! It means love and it means wisdom.

We all know what love means. It's the opposite of hate and of indifference.

Unless you *love* wisdom, you are not really a philosopher. Philosophy is a love affair. There are many famous people in the world who are classified as philosophers, though they should be classified as scholars of philosophy rather than philosophers. Psychologists who study Romeo's love of Juliet, or Dante's love of Beatrice, are not romantic lovers; they are scholars of romantic love. Studying a lion, or a lunatic, or a lover does not make you a lion, or a lunatic, or a lover.

But what is wisdom? The Greeks thought of it as a beautiful woman, a kind of goddess. Their word for it was "Sophia." It's something to fall in love with.

Not all knowledge is wisdom. Memorizing the telephone directory gives you much knowledge but no wisdom.

Wisdom has something to do with values as well as facts. It also has something to do with living as well as thinking. In other words, wisdom is both theory and practice, both a "world-view" and a "life-view," both a set of beliefs about what the real world really is and a set of beliefs about how to live in this world.

For instance, materialists like Marx believe that everything, even human thinking, is made of matter; some schools of Hinduism and Buddhism believe that everything, even the physical world, is made of mind or spirit; and common-sense philosophers like Aristotle and Plato believe that both matter and mind or spirit or soul are real. And this difference in theory makes a difference in practice, in life, in what you take seriously and what you don't.

Take a specific example. Some philosophers, like the Sophist Thrasymachus, whom we will meet as Socrates' main opponent in the

Republic, believe that the way to live successfully (i.e., happily—for happiness is the one thing everyone wants) is to accumulate the material goods of money, pleasure, and power. Others, like Socrates, Plato's teacher, believe that the way to happiness is to cultivate wisdom and virtue in the "deep pockets" of your *soul*.

These are obviously questions that are both very important (for they make a great difference to your life) and very difficult (for most of us do not feel confident that we can *prove* logically that either of the answers is right or wrong and be *certain* of the right answer).

But Socrates does!

It is very useful to read a philosopher who does not simply pat you on the head and affirm what you already believe (like the writers of books you find in airport bookstores, or who appear on Oprah); to read someone who challenges you, fights with you, and makes you fight back with him. It develops your mental muscles, just as boxing with a sparring partner develops the muscles of your arms.

More than that: Philosophy is not just a game for mental exercise. It is practical, in fact it is necessary. If you are running a business, it is important to know the financial resources of your creditors and debtors, but it is even more important to know their philosophy. (That was the mistake of those who invested with Bernie Madoff.) If you are a politician making a treaty with another nation, it is important to know the military power of that nation, but it is even more important to know its philosophy. (That was Chamberlain's mistake at Munich.) If you are marrying someone, it is important, for marital harmony and happiness, to know his or her bathroom habits and bedroom habits, but it is even more important to know his or her philosophy. (That was Macbeth's mistake.)

Philosophy asks questions like these:

(1) What is real and what is not? (metaphysics) E.g., is God real?
(2) What is a human being? (philosophical anthropology) E.g., do we have souls? Do we have free will? What happens when we die?
(3) How can we know when we know the truth? (epistemology) Is science the only reliable method?
(4) What ought we to do? (ethics) E.g., is it ever right to lie?
(5) What is a good society? (political philosophy) E.g., should we encourage democracy for everyone in the world?

(6) Why do we love beauty? (aesthetics) E.g., is "modern art" really ugly?
(7) How should we use words? (philosophy of language and methodology) E.g., should we use a clearer language than ordinary language for philosophy, like mathematical logic?

You can apply philosophy to anything. Thus there is philosophy of history, philosophy of education, philosophy of religion, philosophy of science, philosophy of sexuality, philosophy of music, philosophy of humor, etc.

And it's all in Plato (actually, in Socrates, his teacher and model, who wrote nothing but who inspired Plato's writings). It all started there. So let us start there too.

3. Why is Plato the best introduction to philosophy?

I've taught philosophy for over fifty years now, including one section of a course for beginners almost every semester. I've tried just about everything possible, and a few things that are impossible. I've experimented with every one of the many alternative methods available for teaching beginners. (I have ADD so I get easily bored and like to try new things all the time.) But I've never found anything nearly as successful as Plato.

That's true of writing too. Students are more successful imitating Plato, writing Socratic dialogs, than writing anything else. That's true by their own estimation (most of them say they have the most fun doing it) and by mine (most of those grades are the highest).

That's why I've written two other books to introduce philosophy through Plato: *Philosophy 101 by Socrates: an Introduction to Philosophy via Plato's "Apology"* and *The Platonic Tradition* (a more historical survey).

But why? Why does reading Plato work best?

Well, suppose you could have Newton as your physics teacher, or Shakespeare as your literature teacher, or St. Thomas Aquinas as your theology teacher. Wouldn't that be just a little bit better than having the teacher you have now, even if you have a pretty darn good one?

Well, you *can* have these great geniuses like Newton or Shakespeare or Aquinas as teachers because they did one of the most powerful things a human being can ever do: they wrote great books. Great books are like ghosts: even though their authors are dead and gone from this world, you can still meet them in this world because they left behind their spirits, their minds, though not their physical brains and bodies. They did this by writing books. Books are like ghosts. They can haunt you. They carry other minds into your mind even when those other minds are dead.

Books are the single greatest invention in the history of education, the single most powerful device for communicating the minds of geniuses like Plato to the minds of idiots like you and me. Medicine can't do brain transplants, because we don't have the technology for it; but education can do mind transplants, because we do have the technology for that: books. (Of course, there is no guarantee that these "mind transplants" will "take." That's mainly up to the recipients.)

There are three kinds of books, in every field.

(1) The vast majority of books are useful but forgettable. They are like bread, or milk, or hamburgers.

(2) A minority of books are truly bad books: they are either remarkably stupid, silly, and shallow (these are like cheap candy), or else they are dishonest and lying books, which are like poisons. Hitler's *Mein Kampf, How to Commit Suicide, The Joys of Pederasty, How To Make Your Own Nuclear Bomb and Hold the World Hostage,* and *How To Use A Ouija Board to Meet Satan* are poison books. So is *Fifty Shades of Gray,* unless sadomasochism and the abuse of women is health food for the soul.

(3) An even smaller minority of books are great books. They are like gourmet banquets, like "Babette's Feast" (see the movie!). Great books keep nourishing you every time you reread them. They don't dry up, ever. A great book is like a colossal cosmic cow that gives you fresh milk every morning.

How many great books are there? Probably more than 100 but fewer than 1000.

There are probably ten or twenty *categories* of great books. Philosophy is one of them. If the fifty greatest teachers in the world were to list the ten greatest books in philosophy, I think that Plato's *Republic* would probably be the only book on every single list.

Ralph Waldo Emerson said, "Plato *is* philosophy and philosophy *is* Plato." Alfred North Whitehead (himself a great philosopher) said, "The safest characterization of the history of Western philosophy is that it is a series of footnotes to Plato." The old Professor Digory Kirke in C. S. Lewis's *The Chronicles of Narnia* said: "It's all in Plato, all in Plato. Bless me, what do they teach them in the schools nowadays, anyway?"

Plato is also the best writer in the history of philosophy. Most philosophers are dull, undramatic, abstract writers. (There are a few other exceptions besides Plato: Augustine, Pascal, Nietzsche, Kierkegaard.) But Plato wrote dramatic dialogs, in which Socrates, his famous teacher, interacts with a great variety of fools. These dialogs are like intellectual swordfights, and even though you know Socrates is going to win, they are exciting because you see his ideas come alive, like a sword in the hand of a master. Plato is a great dramatist, a great poet, and a great psychologist as well as a great philosopher. Nobody else who ever lived combined those four talents as well as Plato did.

Socrates was the father of philosophy, the first great philosopher. He wrote nothing—like Jesus, like Buddha. But Plato, his brilliant disciple, did. Plato wrote thirty Socratic dialogs. Some of them (probably the first half) are based on actual conversations Socrates had with real people in his native city of Athens some 2400 years ago. Others are Plato's invention, written after Socrates died, using Socrates as a fictional figure. The *Republic* is probably a mixture of these two things. Book I, about justice in individual lives, is probably genuinely Socratic; the rest, which is highly political, is probably Plato alone.

You hold in your hands a book that will allow you to become an apprentice to Plato. An even better book for that purpose would be the collected dialogs of Plato. That's the next book you should buy, after you finish this one. You can get all thirty dialogs in one hardcover volume for about $40. There are two different versions of it, both good. You can also get seven of Plato's best dialogs, including the whole *Republic* (also *Ion*, *Meno*, *Apology*, *Crito*, *Phaedo*, and *Symposium*) in one cheap little paperback, translated by W. H. D. Rouse and called *Great Dialogs of Plato*.

Apprenticeship to a great master is the best way to learn any art. You will understand what philosophy is better by watching a master do it than by reading abstract definitions of it from a second-rate philosopher like me, or by a mere scholar. Concrete examples are always the easiest way to learn things. Plato's dialogs are the world's first, and still the best, concrete example of philosophizing.

St. Augustine was another great philosopher who, like Plato, combined great love and great brilliance. His *Confessions* is the story of the many passionate loves of his life, such as pleasure, prestige, pride, and power, and the story of his long, winding road of conversion to the God of love and the love of God. But the first step in that conversion, he himself said, came at age 19 from reading a great book by a pagan Roman philosopher, Cicero. It was called *Hortensius,* and it was an introduction to philosophy, "the love of wisdom." Augustine fell totally in love with the first absolute he ever met: wisdom. Not the wisdom of Cicero, or of Plato, not an ideology, but "wisdom itself, wherever it might be." That is what reading Plato's *Republic* can do for you—it can make you fall in love with an absolute—and that is why it can be a great introduction to philosophy.

If philosophy is the love of wisdom, then an introduction to philosophy ought to be a matchmaker, not a textbook. For wisdom (*Sophia*) is a beautiful woman to fall in love with, not a "subject" to master. (What kind of loveless idiot would want to "master" a beautiful woman?)

I introduce you to this love affair through, Plato. I choose Plato because he is a great matchmaker, not mainly because he is an important historical figure. We're studying philosophy here, not history. The study of history is a wonderful means to that end but it is not the end. The history of philosophy is like a gold mine; you go there for the gold, not for the mine. It's where you find the good stuff, the great masters.

Plato is a better teacher than you will ever meet in the land of the living. In fact, Plato still is in the land of the living. He's still alive and kicking in his dialogs. He rubs off on you if you are wise and humble enough to become his student.

What's the alternative to learning philosophy this way? One alternative is a historical survey in which you meet so many philosophers that you do not have the time to meet any one of them in depth, and in which you just learn a summary of the various opinions of each one. That might win you money on a quiz show but it won't make you wise.

Another alternative is the "analytic" or "systematic" approach, which is a survey of logical arguments about abstract issues that only philosophers worry about—like how do we know there is a real world out there at all? In this kind of approach, which is used in most introductory anthologies of philosophy, these issues are uprooted from their history and from the persons who first raised them. Most of the arguments are taken from current professional articles which no one ever fell in love with, and which turn off 90% of all students who have to study them, even though they are good intellectual discipline. Issues and arguments are indispensable, but they are best appreciated in the context of apprenticeship to a great master and reading a great book.

4. Who was Socrates?

You can no more meet Plato without meeting Socrates than you can meet Matthew, Mark, Luke and John without meeting Jesus. The question should really be "Who *is* Socrates," not "Who *was* Socrates?" because he is still alive in Plato's writings, and he can "come alive" to you if you let him. How do you do this? By reading actively rather than passively. Let him challenge you, let him question you, accept your task of having to give him your answers to his questions. And then talk back to him and question him. If you do that, you will find him giving answers to your questions as well as demanding that you give your answers to his. You will find yourself interacting with Plato's literary Socrates almost as you interact with a live person—or his ghost.

Socrates wrote nothing (he'd never get tenure today); but he had disciples, and one of them was a genius who remembered and wrote down some of the philosophical conversations Socrates actually had with many real people in Athens. Scholars disagree about how much Plato added to what Socrates actually said, but all agree that the real historical Socrates appears in Plato's dialogs. (These dialogs were circulated in Plato's lifetime among people who knew the real Socrates, so Plato couldn't get away with much messing with the facts.) After Socrates died, Plato continued to write Socratic dialogs, imagining what

Socrates would have said to a number of more complex, difficult, technical, and abstract questions; but the fictional Socrates in Plato's later dialogs is not nearly as lively, and he sounds more like a philosophy professor in a university (which was what Plato was: he invented the world's first university, the "Academy"). Book I of the *Republic* is probably an authentic early Socratic conversation, but the rest of the *Republic* is probably Plato's later invention, since Socrates never ventured into politics.

Socrates was a new kind of man: the first man in history who very clearly knew what a logical argument was. He seemed to many of his contemporaries to be a wizard with words. He just dazzled and danced around everyone else. Imagine LeBron James playing basketball with twelve-year-olds. The freedom-loving citizens of Athens, the world's first democracy, feared him and misunderstood him so radically that they had him killed for not believing in the gods of the State and for "corrupting the youth" by showing them, by example, how to question everything by his famous "Socratic method" of arguing, like a good cross-examining attorney in court.

Socrates changed the content of philosophy as well as its method: previous philosophers (the "pre-Socratics") had speculated mainly about the universe outside us; Socrates turned philosophy's attention to man and human life, especially good and evil, right and wrong, virtues and vices.

Socrates' constant opponents were the Sophists, a class of thinkers who also argued, but like bad lawyers. They were clever but they did not care about winning the truth, only about winning the argument, and they used any rhetorical tricks or deliberate logical fallacies that worked. They did not believe in objective truth. Protagoras the Sophist is famous for saying that "(the opinion of the individual) man is the measure of all things." They also disbelieved in objective good and evil. They were moral relativists. Thrasymachus, in Book I of the *Republic*, was one of them. Socrates, in contrast, hunted the truth like a passionate pig hunting precious truffles. He was skeptical of most claims to have found the truth, and mercilessly exposed fallacies and refuted illogical arguments, but he was not skeptical of truth itself, even (especially) in moral matters.

Especially interesting are the early Socratic dialogs about values, especially:

Lysis, about friendship

Laches, about courage

Charmides, about self-control

Ion, about rhetoric

Phaedrus, about art and divine inspiration

Philebus, about pleasure

Protagoras, about whether evil is really ignorance

Meno, about teaching and learning

Gorgias, about rhetoric and power versus philosophy and virtue as life's practical goods. The *Gorgias* is essentially the *Republic* without its politics, metaphysics, and epistemology. It is thus the best dialog to read to "get" the main point of the *Republic* from another angle.

Symposium, about love

Euthyphro, about ethics' relation to religion

Crito, about obeying even bad laws

Apology, Socrates' defense of himself and of philosophy at his trial. (Did it work? Well, they killed him, but they couldn't kill philosophy.)

Phaedo, about Socrates facing death

The last eight in this list are the most highly recommended, both for their importance, their logical and literary craftsmanship, and their clarity and intelligibility for beginners.

5. Introduction to the *Republic*

The following selective tour through the long (400 pages!) *Republic* omits or very briefly summarizes most of the political specifics, which are (1) relatively long and boring to read, (2) picky and detailed, (3) controversial if not positively wacky, and (4) often culturally relative and outdated. The *Republic* is indeed about politics, but that's not its main appeal. In fact, few people today would *want* to live in Plato's "ideal" state. But the *Republic* is about much more than politics: it's about who you are and how you should live and how to be happy. It's about justice and injustice and good and evil and truth and falsity. It's about "the meaning of life." It's a whole "world view" and "life view." It's "existential."

Peter Kreeft

Long introductions to a book are usually boring because the reader has no concrete data in front of him yet, since he has not yet read the book. So this introduction will be mercifully short. ("Heeere's Johnny!" is my favorite.)

II. The *Republic*

1. The Beginning: Bringing Philosophy Into Politics

In many of his dialogs Plato plants a hidden clue to their central meaning in the first line. The first line of the *Republic* is: **I went down to the Piraeus yesterday . . .** The "I" here is Socrates and the Piraeus was the rather dirty and humid port of Athens. Athens was the city of the philosophers and artists, which was a beautiful, clean city on a hill. The Piraeus was famous for dirt, disease, corruption, and political deals. Plato is hinting that in this book he will take his fictional Socrates down from Athens to Piraeus, i.e., from philosophy to politics.

Actually, politics is not mentioned at all in Book I, which is probably an actual conversation with the real Socrates, while the rest of the *Republic*, which is more political, is probably purely Plato's invention. Plato's single most important political proposal in the *Republic* is that **philosophers must become kings, or kings become philosophers, and thus political power and wisdom be joined.** The real Socrates never went into politics (he said that "the god" told him not to, and that he feared he would lose his soul if he did), so Plato will now amend that: his fictional Socrates will.

This proposal (to bring the light of philosophy into the darkness of politics) is symbolized by the most famous passage in the *Republic,* in fact the single most famous passage in any book of philosophy ever written, viz the account of "Plato's Cave." The philosopher "goes down" into the "cave" where we, the ignorant, live among shadows, and he liberates us, leads us out of the cave and into the larger world, the light of wisdom. This is forecast in the *Republic*'s first word, **katēben**, "I went down."

What is this wisdom that the philosopher brings to humanity? There are many parts to it, some of which are profoundly difficult, though fascinating (especially "Platonic Ideas" or Plato's "Theory of Forms"); but the main point, the final conclusion of the whole *Republic,* is astonishingly simple and familiar: that **justice is more profitable than injustice.** In other words, moral goodness (justice is the key moral virtue for Plato) always makes you happy and moral badness always makes you miserable.

As we shall see soon, Plato means by "justice" something much more comprehensive than just legal justice, and even something more than just giving others what they deserve, or "giving each his due." He means a virtue or habit of character that includes all the other "cardinal (foundational) virtues" (wisdom, courage, and self-control). He means "righteousness" in general.

That you have to be good to be happy is a platitude taught by almost every moral teacher in history. But Plato claims to prove it conclusively, with certainty, for the first time. And if he succeeds, if he makes us certain of this, then he will change the world, because he will change our lives. For why do we ever do evil or injustice? Only because we think it will bring us some "profit" in happiness. Everyone always seeks happiness. If sin didn't look like fun, we'd all be saints. Well, the *Republic*'s high ambition is to remove that illusion, that ignorance which (Plato believes) is at the root of all evil; to glue the justice we do not always seek to the happiness we do always seek, so that just as we already seek happiness 100% of the time, we will also seek justice 100% of the time. I think no book of philosophy ever had a higher, more noble, more radical goal than this one.

Of course Plato failed, in at least two ways. The political "utopia" or "ideal state" of the *Republic* has not convinced many people. And the moral ideals, even though they are much more popularly accepted, did not in fact make us saints. Many readers are convinced that Plato has indeed proved that justice is always more profitable than injustice, that the only way to be good is to be happy—and yet they are not wholly good, even though they want to be wholly happy. The world knows the *Republic* very well—it is the single most famous book in the history of philosophy—and yet we are not saints. So it didn't change the world.

Or did it? And even if it did fail to convert the world, isn't a noble failure better than an ignoble success? Machiavelli has been more "successful" than Plato; does that mean he's right? It may very well be that Plato is quite right but we are too blind to see it. Keep your mind open on that issue; I raise it not to close your mind but to open it.

2. The Question: What is Justice?

I went down yesterday to the Piraeus with Glaucon the son of Ariston, that I might offer up my prayers to the goddess; and also because I wanted to see in what manner they would celebrate the festival, which was a new thing . . . (327)

In addition to the symbolic significance of the "I went down" (*katēben),* this beginning contains a hint that Socrates is satirizing the Greeks' changing fashions in religion. A new goddess is a logical contradiction, for a god must be eternal and changeless. Socrates (Plato) is going to propose not a new religion but a new *kind* of religion: its absolute(s) will be real, not imagined, and will be truly absolute, not relative to human invention.

The people in this dialog are real people. Glaucon was Plato's brother, and he is the one who "gets" Plato's points best in the *Republic.* Plato is implicitly asking us to identify with Glaucon and calling us his brothers. Ariston was Plato's father. "Ariston" means "the best" or "excellence" ("aristocracy" means literally "rule by the most excellent"), and Plato is implicitly telling us that this "excellence" in wisdom and virtue is our heritage and inheritance too.

Polemarchus the son of Cephalus chanced to catch sight of us from a distance as we were starting on our way home, and told his servant to run and bid us wait for him. The servant took hold of me by the cloak behind, and said: Polemarchus desires you to wait.

I turned round and asked him where his master was.

There he is, said the youth, coming after you, if you will only wait.

Certainly we will, said Glaucon; and in a few minutes Polemarchus appeared, and with him Adeimantus, Glaucon's brother, Niceratus the son of Nicias, and several others who had been at the procession.

Polemarchus said to me: I perceive, Socrates, that you and your companion are already on your way to the city (Athens).

You are not wrong, I said.

But do you see, he rejoined, how many we are?

Of course.

And are you (two) stronger than all these? For if not, you will have to remain where you are.

May there not be the alternative, I said, that we may persuade you to let us go?

But can you persuade us if we refuse to listen to you? he said.

Plato here symbolizes three classical solutions to the fundamental political problem of the inevitable conflict of wills between different groups of people: (1) forcible change ("do you see how many we are?"), (2) the conservative "status quo" ("remain where you are") and (3) rational persuasion, which is Plato's alternative. Its power is like that of light ("the light of reason"); its weakness is our power to shut our eyes ("refuse to listen"). It's up to us whether we will open the eyes of our mind or to Plato's claims to teach rational wisdom.

And "reason" for Plato and the ancients in general means something crucially larger than it means to most people today: not just cleverness but wisdom; not just logic but ethics; not just truths but goods; not just facts but values and virtues. The *Republic* is a work of moral persuasion.

Socrates' three interlocutors in Book I exemplify these three political solutions: Thrasymachus #1, Cephalus #2 and Polemarchus #3. (The accent is on the second syllable in "Thrasymachus," on the first in "Cephalus," and on the third in "Polemarchus.")

We went with Polemarchus to his house; and there we found his brothers Lysias and Euthydemus, and with them Thrasymachus the Chalcedonian . . . There too was Cephalus the father of Polemarchus, whom I had not seen for a long time, and I thought him very much aged. He was seated on a cushioned chair and had a garland on his head, for he had been sacrificing in the court; and there were some other chairs in the room arranged in a semicircle, upon which we sat down by him. He saluted me eagerly, and then he said:

You don't come to see me, Socrates, as often as you ought. If I were able to go and see you I would not ask you to come to me. But at my age I can hardly get to the city, and therefore you should come oftener to the Piraeus. For let me tell you, that the more the pleasures of the body fade away, the greater to me is the pleasure and

charm of conversation. Do not, then, deny my request, but make our house your resort and keep company with these young men. We are old friends, and you will be quite at home with us.

I replied: There is nothing which, for my part, I like better, Cephalus, than conversing with aged men. For I regard them as travelers who have gone a journey which I too may have to go, and of whom I ought to inquire whether the way is smooth and easy or rugged and difficult. And this is a question which I should like to ask of you who have arrived at that time which the poets call the threshold of old age: Is life harder towards the end, or what report do you have to give of it?

I will tell you, Socrates . . . Certainly old age has a great sense of calm and freedom. When the passions relax their hold, then, as Sophocles says, we are freed from the grasp not of one mad master only but of many. The truth is, Socrates, that these regrets, and also the complaints about (sexual) relations, are to be attributed to the same cause, which is not old age but men's characters and temperaments. For he who is of a calm and happy nature will hardly feel the pressure of age, but to him who is of an opposite disposition, youth and age are equally a burden.

I listened in admiration, and wanting to draw him out, that he might go on . . . (329)

He replied . . . To him who is conscious of no sin, sweet hope, as Pindar charmingly says, is the kind nurse of his age. "Hope," he says, "cherishes the soul of him who lives in justice . . . ."

Well said, Cephalus, I replied. But as concerning justice, what is it? To speak the truth and pay your debts? No more than this? And even to this are there not exceptions? Suppose that a friend when in his right mind has deposited arms with me and he asks for them when he is not in his right mind. Ought I to give them back to him? No one would say that I ought, or that I should be right in doing so, any more than they would say that I ought always to speak the truth to one who is in his condition.

You are quite right, he replied.

But then, I said, speaking the truth and paying your debts is not a correct definition of justice.

Quite correct, Socrates, if Simonides is to be believed, said Polemarchus, interrupting.

I fear, said Cephalus, that I must go now, for I have to look after the sacrifices, and I hand over the argument to Polemarchus and the company.

Is not Polemarchus your heir, I said.

To be sure, he answered, and went away laughing to the sacrifices.

The great question "What is justice?," like most great questions, comes up casually in conversation. Old Cephalus (whose name means "head") proves not to be much of a thinker, for as soon as the hard question comes up ("but what *is* justice, anyway?") he goes back to his thoughtless and irrational sacrifices. Socrates has refuted Cephalus' popular definition of justice, and Cephalus will not defend it. But his son Polemarchus will. He is heir to Cephalus' money, but also to the argument, which is more precious than money because it is a road, however long and winding, to the goal of the truth, which is *absolutely* precious, especially when it is truth about justice.

"Justice" (*dīkē* or *dikaiosune*) in Greek meant something whose connotations were large. It was applied not just to (1) decisions in a law court, or even to (2) actions between individuals ("giving each man his due") but also to (3) a character trait of an individual (it might be translated "righteousness," as it often is in the letters of St. Paul) and even applied to (4) the harmony of the universe (the uni-versa, the space-time unity of diverse material things) as manifested in the movements of the stars, and to (5) the harmony in music. In the *Republic* Plato sees musical education as the beginning of education in justice, and therefore takes great pains to make what seems to us ridiculously picky laws about it. Like St. Paul, Plato will see justice as a generic virtue, as including all crucially important virtues, especially wisdom (prudence), courage (fortitude) and moderation (self-control). These will become the "four cardinal virtues" for nearly all philosophers until Machiavelli.

Cephalus is a semi-sympathetic character. Plato portrays him as wise in one sense (his moral values, though not his religious values) but unwise in another sense (he will not defend his values with argument). He is not a *dangerously* unwise character, like the young radical Thrasymachus, who is driven by his blind passions. But it is not old Cephalus but the middle-aged Polemarchus who learns Socrates' wisdom best. He typifies the mean between unthinking conservatism (Cephalus) and unthinking radicalism (Thrasymachus). He thinks, and therefore learns.

So Polemarchus now takes up the argument and tries to defend the popular definition of justice that he quoted from the poet Simonides, that justice is paying your debts. This includes two things: rewarding friends and punishing enemies, giving good to "the good guys" and bad to "the bad guys." This is a child's natural definition of justice.

Socrates will find two problems with it. The first is that it wrongly assumes that we never err about who is good and who is bad. This is easily amended by Polemarchus. But the second problem is more radical. Can what is good do bad to anybody, even enemies? Socrates, 430 years before Jesus, asserts a principle that sounds very much like "Love your enemies; do good to those who harm you." Socrates will claim that justice cannot harm anyone at all, even enemies (though it may punish them, for their own good).

(Socrates asks Polemarchus:) **Tell me then, O heir of the argument, what did Simonides say, and according to you truly say, about justice?**

He said that the repayment of a debt is just, and in saying so he appears to me to be right.

I should be sorry to doubt the word of such a wise and inspired man; but his meaning, though probably clear to you, is the reverse of clear to me. For he certainly does not mean, as we were just now saying, that I ought to return a deposit of arms or of anything else to one who asks for it when he is not in his right senses. And yet a deposit cannot be denied to be a debt.

True . . .

And are enemies also to receive what we owe to them?

To be sure, he said . . . that is to say, evil . . . justice is the art which gives good to friends and evil to enemies . . . (332)

Well, there is another question: By friends and enemies do we mean those who are so really, or only in seeming?

Surely, he said, a man may be expected to love those whom he thinks good, and to hate those whom he thinks evil.

Yes, but do not persons often err about good and evil? Many who are not good seem to be so, and conversely.

That is true.

Then to them the good will be enemies and the evil will be their friends?

True.

And in that case they will be right in doing good to the evil and evil to the good?

Clearly.

But the good are just and would not do an injustice?

True.

Then according to your argument it is just to injure those who do no wrong?

Nay, Socrates, the doctrine is immoral . . . . I think that we had better correct an error into which we seem to have fallen in the use of the words "friend" and "enemy."

What was the error, Polemarchus? I asked.

We assumed that he is a friend who seems to be or who is thought to be good.

And how is the error to be corrected?

We should rather say that he is a friend who is, as well as seems, good; and that he who seems only, and is not good, only seems to be and is not a friend. And of an enemy the same may be said.

You would argue that the good are our friends and the bad our enemies?

Yes.

And instead of saying simply, as we did at first, that it is just to do good to our friends and harm to our enemies, we should further say: It is just to do good to our friends when they are good, and harm to our enemies when they are evil?

Yes, that appears to be the truth.

But ought the just to injure anyone at all?

Undoubtedly he ought to injure those who are both wicked and his enemies.

Socrates loves to doubt what is undoubted. What follows is his purely logical argument for "love your enemies." Socrates is the first person we know of to have taught this.

His argument follows the typical Socratic pattern: (1) It begins with a number of examples that are similar, taken from ordinary experience. (2) It sees in these examples a single general principle. (Aristotle calls this "inductive abstraction," abstracting a general principle from particular examples of it.) (3) It formulates this principle as a necessary and universal truth. (4) It then deduces from it the surprising solution to the original question. Thus we have an implicit epistemology, or theory of knowledge, consisting of (1) sensation, (2) induction, (3) understanding, and (4) deduction. Step (1) sees reasons particulars, (2) "up" from particulars to a universal, (3) sees and understands the universal, and (4) reasons "down" from the universal to the particular.

When horses are injured, are they improved or deteriorated?

The latter.

Deteriorated, that is to say, in the good qualities of horses, not of dogs?

Yes, of horses.

And dogs are deteriorated in the good qualities of dogs but not of horses?

Of course.

And will not men who are injured be deteriorated in that which is the proper virtue of men?

Certainly.

And that human virtue is justice?

To be sure.

Then men who are injured (as men) are of necessity made unjust?

That is the result.

But can the musician by his art make men unmusical?

Certainly not.

Or the horseman by his art make them bad horsemen?

Assuredly not.

Any more than heat can produce cold?

It cannot.

Or drought (produce) moisture?

Clearly not.

Nor can the good harm any one?

Impossible.

And the just is good?

Certainly.

Then to injure a friend, or anyone else, is not the act of a just man, but of the opposite, who is the unjust?

I think what you say is quite true, Socrates.

Then if a man says that justice consists in the repayment of debts, and that good is the debt which a man owes to his friends, and evil the debt which he owes to his enemies—to say this is not wise. For it is not true if, as has been clearly shown, the injuring of another can be in no case just.

I agree with you, said Polemarchus . . . (335)

At this point Thrasymachus interrupts, like a wild bull, faulting Socrates for meekly bowing down to the logic of the argument instead of asserting his superior "will to power." Thrasymachus is a forerunner of both Machiavelli and Nietzsche. No two philosophers have ever been more extreme opposites than Thrasymachus and Socrates. It is almost like seeing Satan and Jesus in dialog.

Several times in the course of the discussion Thrasymachus had made an attempt to get the argument into his own hands, and had been put down by the rest of the company, who wanted to hear the end. But when Polemarchus and I had done speaking and there was a pause, he could no longer hold his peace; and, gathering himself up, he came at us like a wild beast, seeking to devour us. We were quite panic-stricken at the sight of him.

He roared out to the whole company: What folly, Socrates, has taken possession of you all? And why, sillybillies, do you knock under to one another? I say that if you really want to know what justice is, you should not only ask but answer . . .

Thrasymachus, I said with a quiver, don't be hard upon us. Polemarchus and I may have been guilty of a little mistake in the

argument, but I can assure you that the error was not intentional. If we were seeking for a piece of gold, you would not imagine that we were 'knocking under to one another' and so losing our chance of finding it. And why, when we are seeking for justice, a thing more precious than many pieces of gold, do you say that we are weakly yielding to one another and not doing our utmost to get at the truth? Nay, my good friend, we are most willing and anxious to do so, but the fact is that we cannot. And so, you people who know all things should pity us and not be angry with us.

How characteristic of you, Socrates! he replied, with a bitter laugh—that's your ironical style! Did I not foresee? Have I not already told you that whatever he was asked he would refuse to answer? . . .

Thrasymachus, as any one might see, was in reality eager to speak, for he thought that he had an excellent answer, and would distinguish himself. But at first he pretended to insist on my answering. At length he consented to begin.

Behold, he said, the wisdom of Socrates. He refuses to teach himself and goes about hunting from others, to whom he never even says Thank you.

That I learn from others, I replied, is quite true. But that I am ungrateful, I wholly deny. Money I have none, and therefore I pay in praise, which is all I have; and how ready I am to praise anyone who appears to me to speak well, you will very soon find out when you answer. For I expect that you will answer well.

Listen, then, he said; I proclaim that justice is nothing else than the interest of the stronger. And now why do you not praise me? But of course you won't.

Let me first understand you, I replied. Justice, as you say, is the interest of the stronger. What, Thrasymachus, is the meaning of this? You cannot mean to say that because Polydamas the wrestler is stronger than we are and finds the eating of beef conducive to his bodily strength, that to eat beef is therefore equally for our good who are weaker than he is, and right and just for us?

That's abominable of you, Socrates. You take the words in the sense which is most damaging to the argument.

Not at all, my good sir, I said; I am trying to understand them, and I wish that you would be a little clearer.

Well, he said, have you never heard that forms of government differ? There are tyrannies, and there are democracies, and there are aristocracies.

Yes, I know.

And the government is the ruling power in each state.

Certainly.

And the different forms of government make laws democratical, aristocratical, tyrannical, with a view to their several interests. And these laws, which are made by them for their own interests, are the justice which they deliver to their subjects. And him who transgresses them, they punish as a breaker of law, and unjust. And that is what I mean when I say that in all states there is the same principle of justice, which is the interest of the government; and as the government must be supposed to have the power, the only reasonable conclusion is that everywhere there is one principle of justice, which is the interest of the stronger.

Now I understand you, I said. But whether you are right or not I will try to discover . . . . (339)

Socrates takes such pains to define terms carefully because these two things have to come in the right order: first clear understanding and only then certainty about the truth.

Thrasymachus' definition of justice has two aspects, one of which is very unpopular today in Western civilization and the other of which is very popular. The unpopular one is the glorification of force or power. The popular one is called by various names: moral or ethical positivism is the technical term. It means that moral values are "posited" or made or declared or brought into existence by the will of man. Justice is therefore the label that lawmakers pin on the laws they make; and the laws they make. So justice is socially relative, particular, and changeable, not absolute and universal and unchanging. In other words, there is no "natural moral law", no law higher than the laws made ("posited") by man. This is today the almost-official philosophy of the European Union, of nearly all the law schools in America, typified by what is called "critical legal studies" at Harvard, and even of the Supreme Court.

Socrates profoundly disagrees with it. It means, really, that justice is just the mask painted on the face of power, whether this power is democratic or tyrannical, collective or individual. There is no issue that more radically distinguishes our modern Western civilization from all others that have ever existed in the history of the world. Now you see why the *Republic* is such an important and currently relevant book.

You can also see why I have deleted most of its political details: because they are diversions from this main point. Our disagreement with the details of Plato's political preferences, which are definitely aristocratic rather than democratic, and can even be misinterpreted as a kind of benevolent totalitarianism, is a convenient excuse for ignoring this main point.

Thrasymachus next accuses Socrates of naïve altruism:

(No one has) taught you to know the shepherd from the sheep.

What makes you say that, I replied.

Because you fancy that the shepherd or oxherd fattens the sheep or oxen with a view to their own good and not to the good of himself or his master. And you further imagine that the rulers of states, if they are true rulers, never think of their subjects as sheep, and that they are not studying their own advantage day and night . . . . for the unjust is lord over the truly simple and just; he is the stronger, and his subjects do what is for his interest, and minister to his happiness, which is far from being that of their own.

Consider further, most foolish Socrates, that the just is always a loser in comparison with the unjust . . .

For mankind censure injustice because they fear that they may be the victims of it, not because they shrink from committing it . . .

Thrasymachus, when he had thus spoken, having like bathman deluged our ears with his words, had a mind to go away. But the company would not let him. They insisted that he should remain and defend his position. And I myself added my own humble request that he would not leave us.

Thrasymachus, I said, excellent man, how suggestive are your remarks! And are you going to run away before you have fairly

taught or learned whether they are true or not? Is the attempt to determine the way of man's life so small a matter in your eyes—to determine how life may be lived by each one of us to the greatest advantage? (344)

Socrates means by "advantage" not merely "winning" or "satisfying my desires" but "what is truly good for me." This is the main question of the *Republic:* what is a good person and what is a good life? It is not primarily about the political details of "the ideal state" but about how we all should live, about nothing less than "the meaning of life." The two most fundamentally opposite answers to this question will be concretized a little later, by the figures of Socrates vs. Gyges, which are essentially the same as Frodo vs. Gollum (and also Gandalf vs. Sauron) in *The Lord of the Rings.*

Well, then, Thrasymachus, I said, suppose you begin at the beginning and answer me: You say that perfect injustice is more gainful than perfect justice?

Yes, that is what I say . . .

Would you call one of them virtue and the other vice?

Certainly.

I suppose that you would call justice virtue and injustice vice?

What a charming notion! So likely too, seeing that I affirm injustice to be profitable and justice not.

What else, then, would you say?

The opposite, he replied.

And would you call justice vice?

No, I would rather say sublime simplicity.

Then would you call injustice malignity?

No, I would rather say discretion.

And do the unjust appear to you to be wise and good?

Yes, he said; at any rate those of them who are able to be perfectly unjust, and who have the power of subduing states and nations. But perhaps you imagine me to be talking of pickpockets. Even this profession, if undetected, has advantages, though they are not to be compared to those of which I was just now speaking . . . (348)

Socrates now undertakes to refute Thrasymachus' claim.

His starting point is the assumption that things in nature have natural ends, i.e., goods that fulfill their nature. This is an assumption that was part of universal common sense in all cultures, but is questioned by many in our culture today, largely because it is not subject to verification by the scientific method (which of course was not clearly known in Socrates' day). Whether the idea that everything must be tested by the scientific method can itself be tested by the scientific method is a question Socrates may well have asked us moderns if he had lived to meet us.

I will proceed by asking a question: Would you not say that a horse has some end?

I should.

And the end or use of a horse or of anything would be that which could not be accomplished, or not so well accomplished, by any other thing?

I do not understand, he said.

Let me explain. Can you see except with the eye?

Certainly not.

Or hear except with the ear?

No.

These, then, may be truly said to be the end of these organs?

They may.

Can you can cut off a vine-branch with a dagger or with a chisel, and in many other ways?

Of course.

And yet not so well as with a pruning-hook made for that purpose?

True.

May we not say that this is the end of a pruning-hook?

We may.

Then now I think you will have no difficulty in understanding my meaning when I asked the question whether the end of anything would be that which could not be accomplished, or not so well accomplished, by any other thing?

I understand your meaning, he said, and I assent.

And that to which an end is appointed has also an excellence? Need I ask again whether the eye has an end?

It has.

And has not the eye an excellence?

Yes.

And the ear has an end and an excellence also?

True.

And the same is true for all other things: they have each of them an end and a special excellence?

That is so.

Well, can the eyes fulfill their end if they are wanting in their own proper excellence and have a defect instead?

How can they, he said, if they are blind and cannot see?

You mean to say, If they have lost their proper excellence, which is sight. But I have not arrived at that point yet. I would rather ask the question more generally, and only enquire whether the things which fulfill their ends fulfill them by their own proper excellence, and fail of fulfilling them by their own defect?

Certainly, he said.

I might say the same of the ears: when deprived of their own proper excellence they cannot fulfill their end?

True.

And the same observation will apply to all other things?

I agree.

Well, has not the soul an end which nothing else can fulfill? For example, to superintend, and to command, and to deliberate, and the like. Are not these functions proper to the soul, and can they rightly be assigned to any other?

To no other.

And is not life to be reckoned among the ends of the soul?

Assuredly, he said.

And has not the soul an excellence also?

Yes.

And can she, or can she not, fulfill her own ends when deprived of that excellence?

She cannot.

Then a bad soul must necessarily be a bad (Jowett translates *kaka* as "evil," but that has a moral rather than an ontological connotation; Socrates' point is that goodness really *works*) **ruler and superintendent, and the good soul a good ruler?**

Yes, necessarily.

And we have admitted that justice is the excellence of the soul, and injustice the defect of the soul?

That has been admitted.

Then the just soul and the just man will live well, and the unjust man will live ill?

That is what your argument proves.

And he who lives well is blessed and happy, and he who lives ill the reverse of happy?

Certainly.

Then the just is happy and the unjust miserable.

So be it.

But happiness and not misery is profitable.

Of course.

Then, my blessed Thrasymachus, injustice can never be more profitable than justice.

Let this, Socrates, he said, be your banquet at the feast of Bendis. (Jowett: "entertainment at the Bendidea")

For which I am indebted to you, I said, now that you have grown gentle towards me and have left off scolding. Nevertheless, I have not been well feasted. But that was my own fault and not yours. As an epicure snatches a taste of every dish which is successively brought to table, not having allowed himself time to enjoy the one before, so have I gone from one subject to another without having discovered what I sought at first, the nature of justice. I left that enquiry and turned away to consider whether justice is virtue and wisdom or vice and folly; and when there arose a further question about the comparative advantages of justice and injustice, I could not refrain from passing on to that. And the result of the whole discussion has been that I know nothing at all. For I know not (1) what justice is, and therefore I am not likely to know (2)

whether it is or is not a virtue, nor can I say (3) whether the just man is happy or unhappy. (356)

Book I of the *Republic* ends here, a typical Socratic ending. Socrates has refuted Thrasymachus' false definition of justice but not discovered the true one. He is like a garbage man rather than a cook: he removes inedibles but does not supply edibles. But without this preliminary, we would probably mix the two together. And without this preliminary we would not realize how questionable and hard to find this common-sense notion (justice) really is, and would not be motivated to spend more time seeking it.

3. The Deeper Question: How to Live: Socrates vs. Gyges

Book II begins with another hidden clue. It distinguishes what Socrates did for Plato (the kind of thing we find in Book I) and how Plato goes beyond him (the things we find in the rest of the book).

With these words I was thinking that I had made an end of the discussion; but the end, in truth, proved to be only a beginning. For Glaucon, who is always the most pugnacious of men, was dissatisfied at Thrasymachus' retirement. He wanted to have the battle out. So he said to me:

Socrates, do you wish really to persuade us, or only to seem to have persuaded us, that to be just is always better than to be unjust?

I should wish really to persuade you, I replied, if I could.

Then you certainly have not succeeded.

Socrates always insists on poking through appearances to get to reality. This distinction, between appearance and reality, is the source of all philosophy, in fact of all questioning.

Glaucon now begins again by trying to find out what kind of good justice is by dividing all goods into three classes: things that are ends, things that are means, and things that are both. Thrasymachus maintained that justice was only a means to happiness, and that injustice was a superior means. Socrates maintained, against Thrasymachus, that justice was the better means to happiness ("more profitable than injustice"). In the rest of the *Republic* he will prove that it is also an end ("justice is its own reward"), that it is happiness itself.

Let me ask you now—How would you arrange goods? Are there not some which we welcome for their own sakes, and independently of their consequences, as, for example, harmless pleasures and enjoyments, which delight us at the time although nothing follows from them?

I agree in thinking that there is such a class, I replied.

Is there not also a second class of goods, such as knowledge, sight, health, which are desirable not only in themselves but also for their results?

Certainly, I said.

And would you not recognize a third class, such as gymnastic, and the care of the sick, and the physician's art, and also the various ways of money-making? These do us good, but we regard them as disagreeable. And so no one would choose them for their own sakes, but only for the sake of some reward or result which flows from them?

There is, I said, this third class also. But why do you ask?

Because I want to know in which of the three classes you would place justice?

In the highest class, I replied: among those goods which he who would be happy desires both for their own sake and for the sake of their results.

But the many (who agree with Thrasymachus here) **are of another mind. They think that justice is to be reckoned in the troublesome class, among goods which are to be pursued for the sake of rewards and of reputation but in themselves are disagreeable and rather to be avoided.**

The question is crucial. Is morality like medicine or like sex? Is it only *necessary* or is it also *delightful?* Here is the main source of moral evil: the belief that moral virtue is not delightful, or happifying, or "profitable" in itself, only for its rewards. Plato's aim in the *Republic* is nothing less world-shaking than this: to prove to us that this belief is false, and thus to motivate us to fall in love with justice, the key moral virtue, as totally as we now love happiness. So it is not just the radical part of Thrasymachus' philosophy that needs to be refuted (that "might makes right"), which only a minority believe, but most of all the part that is commonly accepted by the majority: that justice is good only as a means, not as an end; for its rewards, not for itself; that it is like medicine, not like sex.

For this reason Glaucon will play devil's advocate and defend Thrasymachus' position more persuasively than Thrasymachus did, hoping that Socrates will give a more persuasive refutation of it than he did in Book I, which did not satisfy even Socrates himself. (See the last paragraph of Book I, in the last section.) It is like the scientific method in setting up a crucial experiment, verifying a theory (Socrates') by the strongest attempts to falsify it.

I know, I said, that this is their manner of thinking, and that this was the thesis which Thrasymachus was maintaining just now when he censured justice and praised injustice. But I am too stupid to be convinced by him.

I wish, said he, that you would hear me as well as him, and then I shall see whether you and I agree. For Thrasymachus seems to me, like a snake, to have been charmed by your voice (refuted by your logic) **sooner than he ought to have been. But to my mind the nature of justice and injustice have not yet been made clear. Setting aside their rewards and results, I want to know what they are in themselves, and how they inwardly work in the soul. If you please, then, I will revive the argument of Thrasymachus.**

First I will speak of the nature and origin of justice according to the common view of them.

Secondly, I will show that all men who practice justice do so against their will, of necessity, but not as a good (in itself).

And thirdly, I will argue that there is reason in this view, for the life of the unjust is after all better far than the life of the just—if what they say is true, Socrates, since I myself am not of that opinion. But still I acknowledge that I am perplexed when I hear the voices

of Thrasymachus and myriads of others dinning in my ears. And, on the other hand, I have never yet heard the superiority of justice to injustice maintained by anyone in a satisfactory way. I want to hear justice praised in respect of itself; then I shall be satisfied. And you are the person from whom I think that I am most likely to hear this. And therefore I will praise the unjust life to the utmost of my power . . . Will you say whether you approve of my proposal?

Indeed I do, nor can I imagine any theme about which a man of sense would oftener wish to converse.

I am delighted, he replied, to hear you say so, and shall begin by speaking, as I proposed, of the nature and origin of justice.

The next paragraph is one of the most important in the *Republic,* for it is the most persuasive and powerful summary of the one thing Plato most wants to refute. In it, I translate *kaka* as "bad" rather than as "evil," since in the context of the argument it means merely "unprofitable" or "unhappifying."

They say that to do injustice is by nature good, and to suffer injustice bad; but that the bad is greater than the good, and so when men have both done and suffered injustice and have had experience of both, not being able to avoid the one (suffering injustice) **and obtain the other** (doing injustice without being punished), **they think that they had better agree among themselves to have neither.** (Modern philosophers, both pessimists like Hobbes and optimists like Rousseau, call this the "social contract" theory of the origin of law.) **Hence there arise laws and mutual covenants. And that which is ordained by law is termed by them lawful and just.**

This they affirm to be the origin and nature of justice. It is a mean or compromise between the best of all, which is to do injustice and not to be punished, and the worst of all, which is to suffer injustice without the power of retaliation. And justice, being at a middle point between the two, is tolerated not as a good (in itself), **but as the lesser evil, and honored by reason of the inability of men to do injustice. For no man who is worthy to be called a man would ever submit to such an agreement if he were able to resist. He would be mad if he did.**

Such is the received account, Socrates, of the nature and origin of justice.

Here's a more concrete way to think of it. Think of two cavemen, Og and Glog, bashing each other over the head with their clubs because they had not yet discovered hockey. Og, who is smarter, says, "Hey, Glog, I got an idea." "What's an 'idea'?" "I just invented it. I'm going to call it 'philosophy.'" "So what's your 'philosophy,' Og?" "That we should both throw away our clubs and stop bashing each other on the head." "But then I couldn't get the pleasure of bashing you." "Right, but you wouldn't get the pain of being bashed back either." "Hmmm . . . I dunno whether that's to my advantage or not. How can I figure that out?" "Look here, Glog: how big is the pleasure you get from bashing me?" "Oh, it's so big! I love it." "And how big is the pain you get when I bash you back?" "Ooooh, it's sooooo big. I hate it." "See? The pain is bigger than the pleasure." "Wow, that's clever, Og. What do you call that—measuring the size of things?" "Math. I just invented it." "So let's see . . . it would pay me to give up the pleasure because then I wouldn't have the pain." "Good thinking, Glog. You just invented logic." "Wow. Wait a minute. I got an even better idea. You do things your way and I'll do things my way. You throw away your club if you want, but I won't." "No, I won't do that. I won't throw away my club unless you throw away yours too." "Awww . . . okay." "See? We just invented something else: contracts." "But how are we going to remember it?" "Let's write it on the wall of the cave." "What's writing?" "I just invented that too." "Wow, Og, you're really smart. What shall we call it?" "Let's call it a law. Yeah, I just invented that too." "But when the rest of the tribe see us throwing away our clubs, they'll all bash us and we won't be able to bash them back." "Right. So we have to persuade them to do the same thing." "How we gonna do that?" "I'll prove it to them as I proved it to you. By that thing I just invented: logic." "But if we all throw away our clubs, the other tribes will kill us." "Yeah, so we have to invent cops." "What's cops?" "Well, we take all our clubs and give them to the ten strongest guys in the tribe, and they'll give them back to us if another tribe invades. And if they don't invade, the cops get to keep all the clubs, and they can kill whoever they see stealing a club and killing somebody else in our tribe."

"Yeah, they'll like that. But what if all the cops are asleep at once? What's to stop somebody from stealing a club and getting his jollies without being clubbed back?" "We gotta invent one more thing." "What?" "Religion." "What's that?" "Gods." "What are gods?" "Invisible cops in the sky who see everything. And if they see anybody killing and getting away with it, they'll punish them really really bad when they die and go into the sky where the gods are." "Do you think people will actually believe that?" "Sure, just watch." And Og was successful, and his tribe flourished because they didn't kill each other, while the other tribes kept killing each other off and perished, and guess which tribe Natural Selection arranged for us to be born from?

Why is this account of the origin of moral law so charming? Because it's so simple. No mysterious thing called conscience in the subjective soul, and in the realm of objective reality no mysterious realm of moral absolutes. This account of the origin of morality obeys the principle of parsimony, or Ockham's Razor ("always use the simplest explanation, the one with the fewest presuppositions"), which is a basic principle of the scientific method. Of course, using it to explain morality assumes without proof that not just science should be done by the scientific method but also morality, and philosophy, and religion, and life, and common sense, and everything else—which assumption, as noted before, cannot be proved by the scientific method. But despite this logical problem, such a "reductionistic" explanation is still charming and attractive, and therefore popular, both in Socrates' day and in ours.

An essential part of this reductionistic and cynical explanation of the origin of justice and morality is the psychological claim that all men are selfish and act unselfishly only because of the fear of punishment. In other words, the inner cop (conscience) is far weaker than the outer cop. As Machiavelli puts it, "the pangs of conscience are far weaker than the fear of punishment." So Glaucon tells the story of Gyges and his magic ring, a story so strikingly similar to the story of Gollum in Tolkien's *The Lord of the Rings* that the borrowing is evident. The ring gives Gyges/Gollum two things: power and invisibility, i.e., the escape from punishment. Glaucon's point is Sauron's prediction that no one, no matter how just, will refuse to use the ring if only he can possess it. In other words, all men believe that perfect injustice, which is not punished, is more profitable than justice; that everyone knows that the main point of Plato's *Republic* is false. If Glaucon were arguing today he would probably say: Look at those who get something like Gyges' ring today, namely the rich and famous especially rock stars or actors. The vast majority of them are corrupted by this power, and devote it not to virtue but to indulgence in vices: promiscuity, drugs, and lives devoted to selfish pleasure. How many of them reach old age?

Now, that those who practice justice do so involuntarily (reluctantly) **and because they do not have the power to be unjust** (and get away with it) **will best appear if we imagine something of this kind: Having given both to the just and the unjust power to do what they will, let us watch and see whither desire will lead them. Then we shall discover, in the very act, the just and unjust man to be proceeding along the same road, following their interest, which all natures deem to be their good, and are only diverted into the path of justice by the force of law.**

The liberty which we are supposing may be most completely given to them in the form of such a power as is said to have been possessed by Gyges, the ancestor of Croesus the Lydian. According to the tradition, Gyges was a shepherd in the service of the king of Lydia. There was a great storm, and an earthquake made an opening in the earth in the place where he was feeding his flock. Amazed at the sight, he descended into the opening, where, among other marvels, he beheld a hollow brazen horse, having doors, at which he, stooping and looking in, saw a dead body of (gigantic) stature, as appeared to him more than human, and having nothing on but a gold ring. This he took from the finger of the dead and reascended.

Now the shepherds met together, according to custom, that they might send their monthly report about the flocks to the king. Into their assembly he came, having the ring on his finger. And as he was sitting among them he chanced to turn the collet of the ring inside his hand, when instantly he became invisible to the rest of the company, and they began to speak of him as if he were no longer present. He was astonished at this, and again touching the ring he turned the collet outwards and reappeared. He made several trials of the ring,

and always with the same result: when he turned the collet inwards he became invisible; when outwards, he reappeared.

Whereupon he contrived to be chosen one of the messengers who were sent to the court, where, as soon as he arrived, he seduced the queen, and with her help conspired against the king and slew him, and took the kingdom.

Suppose now that there were two such magic rings, and the just put on one of them and the unjust the other. No man can be imagined to be of such an iron nature that he would stand fast in justice. No man would keep his hands off what was not his own when he could gladly take what he liked out of the market, or go into houses and lie with anyone at his pleasure, or kill or release from prison whomever he would, and in all respects be like a god among men. Then the actions of the just would be as the actions of the unjust; they would both come at last to the same point.

And this we may truly affirm to be a great proof that a man is just, not willingly or because he thinks that justice is any good (profit) **to him individually** (personally), **but of necessity** (fear of punishment). **For whenever anyone thinks that he can safely be unjust, there he is unjust. For all men believe in their hearts that injustice is far more profitable to the individual than justice; and he who argues as I have been supposing will say that they are right. If you could imagine anyone obtaining this power of becoming invisible and never doing any wrong or touching what was another's, he would be thought by the multitude to be a most wretched idiot—although they would praise him to one another's faces and keep up appearances with one another from a fear that they too might suffer injustice.**

Glaucon now proposes the thought-experiment of comparing not two concrete men, who are mixtures of justice and injustice, but two ideally perfect specimens: the perfectly just and the perfectly unjust. Most men are mixed: "there's a little good in the worst of us and a little bad in the best of us," so we have mixed motives most of the time. But if we could compare the man who has nothing but justice and no power at all (i.e., Socrates!) with the man who has unlimited power (i.e., Gyges with his ring), we could judge which way of life, justice or injustice, was more profitable. The thought experiment is of course "unrealistic," since Plato's portrait of Socrates is probably idealized and Gyges is wholly fictional, not real. Yet this thought experiment is about the very real question: How shall we then live? What is the road to the happiness that all seek, both the good and the evil?

A Christian would substitute Christ for Socrates and Satan for Gyges, and ask the question this way: What does it profit a man if he gains the whole world and loses his own soul?—not just in the next life but in this one? Satanists always have the same motive: power. And this is no lie: as Gandalf says in *The Lord of the Rings,* "I am Gandalf the White, but Black is mightier still!" Saints get martyred, sinners get filthy rich. Is Job the Righteous *happy* there on his dung heap? Is Alexander the Great unhappy after conquering the whole world? The Christian answer is as startling as the Socratic one: yes.

Now if we are to form a real judgment of the life of the just and unjust, we must isolate them. There is no other way. And how is the isolation to be effected? I answer: Let the unjust man be entirely unjust and the just man entirely just. Nothing is to be taken away from either of them, and both are to be perfectly furnished for the work of their respective lives:

First, let the unjust be like other distinguished masters of craft, like the skillful pilot or physician, who knows intuitively his own powers and keeps within their limits, and who, if he fails at any point is able to recover himself. So let the unjust make his unjust attempts in the right way, and lie hidden if he means to be great in his injustice (for he who is found out is nobody). For the highest reach of injustice is to be deemed just when you are not. Therefore I say that in the perfectly unjust man we must assume the most perfect injustice. There is to be no reduction, but we must allow him, while doing the most unjust acts, to have acquired the greatest reputation for justice. If he has taken a false step, he must be able to recover himself. He must be able to speak with great effect, if any of his (evil) **deeds come to light, and he can force his way, where force is required, by his courage and strength, and command of money and friends.**

And at his side let us place the just man in his nobleness and simplicity, wishing (as Aeschylus says) to be good, not to seem good. There must be no seeming; for if he seems to be just, he will be honored and rewarded, and then we shall not know whether he is just for the sake of justice or for the sake of honors and rewards. Therefore let him be clothed in justice only, and have no other covering. And he must be imagined in a state of life opposite the other. Let him be the best of men and let him be thought the worst. Then he will have been put to the proof, and we shall see whether he will be affected by the fear of infamy and its consequences. And let him continue thus to the hour of death: being just and seeming to be unjust.

This man is, of course, Socrates himself. Thus Plato's *Republic* is the fuller "Apology" or "Defense of Socrates." The following sentence is Plato's summary of the whole point and plot of the *Republic*):

When both have reached the uttermost extreme, the one of justice and the other of injustice, let judgment be given which of them is the happier of the two . . . (361)

Adeimantus then adds:

Parents and tutors are always telling their sons and their wards that they are to be just, but why? Not for the sake of justice but for the sake of appearance and reputation . . . .For what men say is that if I am really just but am not also thought to be just, profit there is none . . . but if, though unjust, I acquire the reputation of justice, a heavenly life is promised to me. Since, then, as the philosophers (i.e., the Sophists) **prove, appearance tyrannizes over truth and is lord of happiness, to appearance I must devote myself.** (365)

As Machiavelli says, "few men see what you really are, but all men see what you appear to be." Therefore, in life as in advertising, "image is everything."

If Socrates can change this common opinion, he can change lives. For the only reason we choose evil and injustice is that we believe it will make us happy. If sin didn't look like fun, we'd all be saints. Socrates wants to *prove* to us, not just preach to us, that we are wrong.

The universal voice of mankind is always declaring that justice and virtue are honorable, but grievous and toilsome; and that the pleasures of vice and injustice are easy of attainment, and are only censured by law and opinion . . . they are quite ready to call wicked men happy . . . (364)

No one has ever blamed injustice or praised justice except with a view to the glories, honors, and benefits which flow from them. No one has ever adequately described either in verse or prose the true essential nature of either of them abiding in the soul and invisible to any . . . eye, or shown that of all the things of a man's soul which he has within him, justice is the greatest good (profit), **and injustice the greatest evil (harm). Had this been the universal teaching, had they sought to persuade us of this from our youth upwards, we would not have been on the watch to keep one another from doing wrong, but everyone would have been his own watchman, because afraid, if he did wrong, or harboring in himself the greatest of evils . . . I want to hear from you the opposite side . . .** (367)

4. Societies as Mirrors of Souls

In agreeing to meet this challenge, Plato's Socrates must give us the world's first map of the soul, the world's first psychology. But this is difficult, because the soul is invisible and subjective and individual. If we could find something visible and objective and collective that had the same structure and the same powers as the soul, this would be an effective aid. That thing is the State, which is created by human souls and mirrors human souls. That is why Plato goes into politics in the *Republic:* not as an end but as a means to a psychology which in turn is a means to prove that justice is always more profitable than injustice.

Seeing, then, I said, that we are no great wits, I think that we had better adopt a method which I may illustrate thus: Suppose that

a short-sighted person had been asked by someone to read small letters from a distance, and it occurred to someone else that these same letters might be found in another place which was larger and in which the letters were larger. If they were the same, and he could read the larger letters first and then proceed to the lesser, this would have been a rare piece of good fortune.

Very true, said Adeimantus, but how does the illustration apply to our enquiry?

I will tell you, I replied. Justice, which is the subject of our enquiry, is, as you know, sometimes spoken of as the virtue of an individual, and sometimes as the virtue of a state.

True, he replied.

And is not a state larger than an individual?

It is.

Then in the larger enquiry the quantity of justice is likely to be larger and more easily appear in the state, and secondly in the individual, proceeding from the greater to the lesser and comparing them.

That, he said, is an excellent proposal.

5. Plato's Ideal Society

We will summarize the next few books of the *Republic* much more briefly, instead of using long quotations, since (1) there are too many details to argue about; (2) the details of Plato's "just state" are far more controversial and less influential than his psychology of the individual soul; (3) there is not as much personal drama or "existential" interest as in the discussion of the main question, above, (4) the style is less arresting, and (5) the points of content are clear and easily summarizable. Not until we get to the question about the nature of the philosopher-king in Books 5–7 do we find difficult and profound metaphysical points that both require and reward much commentary.

Here are the main points:

1. Plato believes, and explicitly says, that states get their structure from souls, not vice versa, as in Marxism. States are made in the image of men before men are made in the image of states.

2. Like Marxists, he has a progressive or evolutionary view of the history of states, so he traces their evolving structure through their origin and history as they get more complex and more sophisticated.

3. The origin of the most primitive state is an inherent feature of human nature: that we are not all equal, but different people are good at different things. Thus the origin of the state is natural specialization. Some men excel at farming, others at hunting, others at shelter-building, others at clothes-making. So instead of each man or family doing all four things and doing three of them poorly, the farmers farm for all of them, the hunters hunt for all of them, etc. However, this is still a simple one-class society; all are producers (and consumers).

4. This system of specialization works so well that eventually luxuries are created, which provoke envy and competition and fighting. Thus a warrior class is needed to keep order. This is a two-class society.

5. Warriors, however, are not especially intelligent, and need supervision. Thus a third class has to emerge: the wise, the intellectuals, who educate the warriors. We thus have, by nature rather than a devised "social contract," a three-class society, the classes corresponding to the three needs or social functions: lawmakers (whom Plato calls the "guardians"), law enforcers (the "auxiliaries"), and law abiders (the "producers," the general populace).

6. Each class needs a special virtue. The producers need moderation (not too much and not too little of anything) in both producing and consuming their work; the warriors need courage; and the lawmakers need wisdom. (Actually, Plato says, moderation is needed in everyone in every class.)

7. Justice is the harmony and integration of all three classes in the state (and also, as we shall shortly see, all three virtues in the soul), each doing his own natural and proper work, or "minding his own business." The state, then (the "body politic"), is like the physical body: a natural organism with each organ doing the work it is by nature designed to do.

8. Plato adds some details about the education of the rulers, which he will expand in Book 7. It begins, in early childhood, with music and gymnastics, which put harmony into the sub-rational soul and body as a kind of fertilizer or conditioning for the higher, more rational harmony that will come later.

9. Plato adds elaborate details about the kind of music that is fit for each class, which, he says, should be determined by the lawmakers, the sages. He combines a profound psychology of the power of music over souls, and therefore lives, with a naïve and patronizing, if not totalitarian, desire that this power be dictated by the few, not left up to the free choice of the many. There is reason for this, however: Plato sees the power of music as we see the power of the military. We do not long for or tolerate private armies, or private nuclear arsenals.

10. Plato also launches into a detailed critique of his existing state religion, whose gods are terrible role models since they reflect all the vices of their human inventors. Athens was so ashamed of executing Socrates for the crime of not believing in the gods of the state that Plato could now get away with this radical critique of the official religion of the state in the name of the higher principles of Socratic reasoning.

11. This is at the same time a critique of literature in education, since all the arts, in ancient cultures, had a religious sanction and, often, explicitly religious themes. For Plato, literature should consist of morally true myths or fables rather than morally false ones (like the Homeric gods), especially the "noble lie" that all three classes of the state are children of a single Mother Earth ruled by a wise Fate that decrees their class membership. This will make them all identify with the common good and make them a unified organic community.

12. Plato wants the "state" to monitor education, religion, music, and literature, and will even (in Book 5) advocate the abolition of private families and marriages, like classic Marxism. Yet even though almost no one today agrees with Plato here, it is somewhat unfair, inaccurate and simplistic to call Plato a totalitarian, for at least three reasons: (1) These radical proposals apply only to the few rulers, not the general population. It is like celibacy part of specialized seminary training for priests. (2) The explicit aim is not a concentration of power in the rulers but the common good of the populace. (3) It is not the bureaucratic political modern-style "state," but the small local community, the city-state (*polis*), that he gives these powers to, a community in which everyone knows almost everyone. He explicitly says this society, like a human body, cannot grow beyond its small organic limit.

13. Having found justice in the state, Plato then finds a mirror image of it in the individual soul. As the state has three powers, located in its three natural classes, so the soul has three powers, or faculties: the mind, or reason; the "spirited part," which is a primitive concept of the will (Plato calls it the capacity for the passion of righteous indignation); and the appetites, desires, or passions.

14. Plato arrives at this three-part psychology (which has become almost the standard model for nearly all other psychological systems, e.g., Freud's super-ego, ego and id) by reflecting on the experienced data of inner conflict. Something (desires) pulls us in one direction ("steal that meat!") and something else (reason) pulls us in the opposite direction ("no, don't do it, it's unjust and unwise"), and a third force (the will) settles this dispute by siding either with the passions or with the reason.

15. Each of these inner powers of the soul needs a special virtue: minds need wisdom, wills need courage, and appetites need moderation, or balance, or temperance, or self-control.

16. As in the state, so in the soul, justice is the harmonization and ordering of each of the other three virtues; justice consists in each power in the soul, as each class in the state, doing its own proper and natural work. Thus justice is to the soul what health is to the body: a kind of natural cooperation among the different organs. And this is obviously more "profitable" than injustice, as health is more profitable than disease. We can see this even though we have not yet explored the forms of injustice. But we will see it more clearly when we do that, in Book 8, which describes four forms of injustice in the state, and in Book 9, which describes four corresponding forms of injustice in the soul.

Which is the more profitable: to be just and act justly and practice virtue, whether seen or unseen of gods and men, or to be unjust and act unjustly, if only unpunished and unreformed?

In my judgment, Socrates, the question has now become ridiculous. We know that when the bodily constitution is gone, life is no longer endurable, though pampered with all kinds of meats and drinks and having all wealth and power. And shall we be told that when the very essence of the vital principle (the soul) is undermined and corrupted life is still worth living to a man if only he be allowed

to do whatever he likes, with the single exception that he is not to acquire justice and virtue or to escape from injustice and vice, assuming them both to be such as we have described?

Yes, I said, the question is, as you say, ridiculous. Still, as we are near the spot at which we may see the truth in the clearest manner with our own eyes, let us not faint by the way.

Certainly not, he replied.

Come up hither, I said, and behold the various forms of vice—those of them, I mean, which are worth looking at.

I am following you, he replied. Proceed.

I said: The argument seems to have reached a height from which, as from some tower of speculation, a man may look down and see that virtue is one but the forms of vice are innumerable. There are four special cases which are deserving of note.

What do you mean? he said.

I mean, I replied, that there appear to be as many forms of the soul as there are distinct forms of the state.

What are they?

The first, I said, is that which we have been describing (the just state), and which may be said to have two names, monarchy and aristocracy, according as rule is exercised by one distinguished man or many.

True, he replied.

But I regard the two names as describing one form only; for whether the government is in the hands of one or many, if the governors have been trained in the manner which we have supposed, the fundamental laws of the state will be maintained.

That is true, he replied.

Such is the good and true city or state, and the good and true man is of the same pattern. And if this is right, every other is wrong. And the evil is one which affects not only the ordering of the state but also the regulation of the individual soul, and is exhibited in four forms.

What are they? he said.

I was proceeding to tell the order in which the four evil forms appeared to me to succeed each other, when Polemarchus, who was

sitting a little way off, just beyond Adeimantus, began to whisper to him. Stretching forth his hand, he took hold of the upper part of his coat by the shoulder and drew him towards him, leaning forward himself so as to be quite close and saying something in his ear of which I only caught the words, "Shall we let him off, or what shall we do?"

Certainly not, said Adeimantus, raising his voice.

Who is it, I said, whom you are refusing to let off?

You, he said . . . . What sort of community of women and children is this which is to prevail among our guardians? (449)

This diversion is the most notorious and infamous part of the *Republic.* Plato's philosophy of women is almost guaranteed to offend everyone today. On the one hand, he is a "unisexist" and believes that there are no natural or innate differences between men and women. On the other hand, he believes that women are inferior to men in everything! Many of the very greatest philosophers, throughout history, have said amazingly ridiculous things about the three things most people are the most passionate about and make the most jokes about: sex, religion, and politics.

In contrast, it is Plato's metaphysics and epistemology that are the most famous, the most lasting, and the most challenging points in every age. And these deeper points emerge when Plato asserts that the just state must be ruled by the philosopher, and then proceeds to define the philosopher in terms of epistemology (how he knows: by reason, not just sensation) and metaphysics (what he knows: true being as distinct from becoming). This will be done in the central section of the *Republic,* Books 5–7.

6. Plato's Psychology

Plato is the first person in history to have given us a psychograph, a map of the human soul. In that sense he is the world's first theoretical psychologist.

He clearly teaches the priority of souls over states (1) because souls create states before states form souls (2) and because souls, unlike states, are immortal. Thus all the political details in the *Republic* are means to the end of the psychology. That is clear from the beginning of Book 2, where Socrates proposes the detour into politics not for its own sake but for the sake of understanding souls.

The key idea in both psychology and politics for Plato is natural hierarchy. The just soul is one which is ruled by truth and goodness, and which then, under this higher rule, rules the body, and, through the body, the world. Within the just soul, reason rules the passions through the mediating power of the will, or "the spirited part," which, unlike the passions, accepts reason and enforces it, though it does not originate reason, as the intellect does. To reverse this hierarchy is chaos: it would mean the material world ruling man instead of man ruling the world; and within man it would mean the body ruling the soul instead of the soul ruling the body; and within soul it would mean the passions ruling reason instead of the reason ruling the passions, and "the spirited part" siding with the passions rather than with the reason. Finally, this upside down hierarchy would mean man's mind ruling truth rather than truth ruling his mind; i.e., it would mean rationalization instead of reason, reducing truth to "what I want." (Does this sound familiar?)

Equally opposed to this natural hierarchy is equality: the equality of all idea, even though some ideas conform to truth more than others do; the equality of all the passions, even though some are approved by reason more than others are; and the equality of the soul and the body even though the soul is the very life and ruler of body.

Plato sees the same two patterns of justice and injustice in the state. Justice is the rule of truth through the philosopher-kings, and the wise and benevolent rule of the philosopher-kings over the masses through the "auxiliaries" (who probably include both literal soldiers and writers, or intellectual soldiers). The equality of the three classes would only cause confusion, like each organ in the body trying to do the same work as each other organ.

Thus emerge the "four cardinal virtues" for both souls and states:

(1) justice, the harmony of the whole, each part doing its proper work;

(2) practical wisdom, or directing wisdom, or prudence, in the intellect and in the "guardians" (for the philosopher-kings or "guardians" are to the state what the intellect is to the soul);

(3) courage in the "spirited part" (and in the "auxiliaries"); and

(4) moderation or temperance or self-control in the passions (and in the "producers," the masses, in the state).

The four cardinal virtues, together with the Ten Commandments, have been the most basic moral foundation for Western civilization ever since.

Plato calls the philosopher-kings "guardians" rather than "rulers" because they exist for the welfare of the people, not for their own sake or for power. Since the whole soul depends on the light of reason and since the whole state depends on the wisdom of these "guardians," it is crucial to understand who they are, why they are wise, what gives them the right to rule. Thus in Book 5-7 Plato takes a long detour into the subject of the nature of the ideal philosopher and how he differs from everyone else, what he knows that no one else knows.

And the answer to this question is the single most famous idea in Plato, Plato's "big idea," which is usually called Plato's "theory of Ideas" or "Platonic Ideas," or "Platonic Forms." Plato believes that Justice, and Beauty, and Human Nature, and Redness, and Triangularity, and Horseness are just as real as (and, in fact, in a sense more real than) just actions and beautiful things and particular human beings and red things and all the triangles ever drawn and all the many different horses in the world. Take a deep breath, for we now emerge from cave and into another, larger world.

7. Plato's Metaphysics: the "Theory of Forms" or "Platonic Ideas"

But (the reader may well object) isn't the *Republic* about ethics and politics, about just and unjust states and souls? Those are very concrete and practical and personal matters. Why must Plato now go off on a tangent into the supremely abstract, theoretical, and impersonal areas of philosophy, into metaphysics? Metaphysics is the division of philosophy that asks "What is real?" and what is "reality," or "being"? It does not leave a physical and study only the spiritual or the supernatural, but does "beyond physics" in universality and scope.

Plato turns to metaphysics now because metaphysics is not a tangent at all, but the center, or the foundation, for everything else in philosophy.

Because the most fundamental differences in ethics (and politics, or social ethics) are always rooted in differences in metaphysics. Because "goodness" and "being" cannot be separated. Because ultimately, the most real thing of all is The Good. Because the linguistic distinction between these two, between "is" and "ought," or between "facts" and "values" (very tricky and easily misleading terms!), does not mean a real separation between being and goodness or between metaphysics and ethics.

To see this, look at the question Glaucon, playing devil's advocate for the popular position of Thrasymachus, asks Socrates at the beginning of Book 2: Your picture of the good life, of justice, may be a beautiful and noble *ideal* or *idea*, but is it *real?* Is it realistic? Isn't your philosophy simply your own personal opinions, a set of ideas inside your mind, subjective? Can you show that it is grounded in the nature of objective reality, that it goes "all the way down" or (to change the image) "all the way up" to ultimate reality? That it is (a) objective, (b) universal, holding for all men, times, places, and cultures, (c) unchangeable, and (d) necessary, rather than (a) subjective, (b) particular and personal, (c) changeable, and (d) contingent on human wills?

But to ask this question, to ask whether Socrates' ethics is "realistic" or is instead "a mere ideal," is to ask a metaphysical question. For it implies two questions about what is "real": (1) what is meant by the term "real," and (2) what things have this "realness," what kinds of things are "real"? Are ethical ideals "real" or should they be contrasted with what is "real" because the only things that are "real" are things we sense, concrete things and events in time which are particular, changeable, and contingent? And this is not only *a* metaphysical question but *the* metaphysical question, the very basic question of metaphysics: what is reality, what is being, what is it to "be"?

This metaphysical question also necessarily involves the fundamental epistemological question "What is knowing?" or "How do we know?" For being and knowing imply each other: all being you can possibly refer to is known being, and all knowledge must be knowledge of some being.

It also involves the fundamental question of philosophical anthropology, "What is man?" For what man should be and do (ethics) and what man can know (epistemology) depend on what man is, on what kind of being man participates in. Is he a god (or God) in disguise, or an archangel in drag, or a ghost in a machine, or a psychosomatic (body-and-soul), hylomorphic (matter-and-form) unity, or an ape in a lab coat, or a brain in a vat, or a chemical equation, or a social convention, or a random evolutionary belch from a primordial slime pool?

So we should be sure we understand the contrasting world- and life-views of Socrates and of Thrasymachus. For the populace, in ancient Athens as well as in contemporary America, tend to agree with Thrasymachus' moral relativism and its metaphysical foundation even if they shrink from his Machiavellian focus on power.

Metaphysically, the difference is that for Socrates, there are three worlds, or three kinds of reality, while for Thrasymachus there are only two (or, if he is a materialist, only one). In other words, Socrates is saying to Thrasymachus what Hamlet said to Horatio: "There are more things in heaven and earth than are dreamed of in your philosophy." Not just more things but more *kinds* of things.

Another way to put this is that Thrasymachus is a naturalist while Socrates is a supernaturalist. What that means is that for Thrasymachus the "real" world is simply the world we can see and touch (and perhaps also the inner world of our thoughts and feelings and touchings *of* this objectively real material world). But for Socrates (Plato) there is a third "world," a third kind of reality, which is neither (1) objective and material nor (2) subjective and spiritual but (3) objective and spiritual.

Here is how Plato's metaphysics and epistemology emerges from the argument about politics in the *Republic.*

The single most important practical plank in Plato's political program comes at the exact middle Of the *Republic* (473):

Until philosophers are kings, or the kings and princes of this world have the spirit and power of philosophy, and political greatness and wisdom meet in one, and those commoner natures who pursue either to the exclusion of the other are compelled to stand aside, cities will never have rest from their evils—no, nor the human race, as I believe. And then only will this our state have a possibility of life and behold the light of day . . .

This seems truly absurd. For if Plato is saying that the only hope for America is that philosophy departments should move into the Oval Office, he is a candidate for a nice room in an insane asylum (which is what the country would soon turn into if his proposal were put into practice). But he is speaking of a small community like Athens, not about an enormous artificial entity like America; and above all he is speaking of a real philosopher like Socrates, a truly wise man, not intellectual prostitutes like myself. And that is the next thing he must define: what is a true philosopher?

His first definition of the philosopher is that he is a universalist rather than a specialist; that he has genuine knowledge because his mind is in touch with the one Idea or essence or absolute (such as beauty itself or justice itself) while the non-philosopher only has opinion because his mind is only in touch with the many things that participate in the essence, e.g., things that are only relatively beautiful or just.

Let me ask: Does he who desires any class of goods desire the whole class or a part only?

The whole.

And may we not say of the philosopher that he is a lover not of a part of wisdom only, but of the whole?

Yes, of the whole . . .

Whereas he who has a taste for every sort of knowledge and who is curious to learn and is never satisfied, may be justly termed a philosopher? Am I not right?

Glaucon said: If curiosity makes a philosopher, you will find many a strange being will have a title to the name . . . . Who then are the true philosophers?

Those, I said, who are lovers of the vision of truth.

That is also good, he said, but I should like to know what you mean . . . . How do you distinguish them?

The lovers of sounds and sights, I replied, are, as I conceive, fond of fine tones and colors and forms and all the artificial products that are made out of them, but their mind is incapable of seeing or loving absolute beauty . . . And he who, having a sense of beautiful things, has no sense of absolute beauty, or who if another lead him to a

knowledge of that beauty is unable to follow—of such a one I ask: Is he awake or in a dream only? Reflect: is not the dreamer, sleeping or waking, one who confuses different things, who puts the copy in place of the real object?

I should certainly say that such a one was dreaming.

But take the case of the other, who recognizes the existence of absolute beauty and is able to distinguish the Idea from the objects which participate in the Idea, neither putting the objects in the place of the Idea nor the Idea in place of the objects—is he a dreamer or is he awake?

He is wide awake.

And may we not say that the mind of the one who knows has knowledge, and that the mind of the other, who opines only, has opinion?

Certainly . . .

Does he who has knowledge know something or nothing?

He knows something.

Something that is or is not?

Something that is; for how can that which is not ever be known?

And are we assured, after looking at the matter from many points of view, that absolute being is or may be absolutely known, but that the utterly non-existent is utterly unknown?

Nothing can be more certain.

Good. But if there be anything which is of such a nature as (at the same time both) to be (real) and not to be (real), that will have a place intermediate between pure being (reality) and the absolute negation of being?

Yes, between them.

And, as knowledge corresponded to being, and ignorance . . . to non-being, there has to be discovered, for that intermediate between being and not-being, a corresponding intermediate between ignorance and knowledge?

Certainly.

Do we admit the existence of opinion?

Undoubtedly.

As being the same as knowledge, or another faculty (power)?

Another faculty.

Then opinion and knowledge have to do with different kinds of (subject) matter, corresponding to this difference of faculties?

Yes.

And knowledge is relative to being and knows being . . . And do we know what we opine? Or is the subject-matter of opinion the same as the subject matter of knowledge?

Nay, he replied, that has already been disproven, if difference in faculty implies difference in the sphere or subject-matter, and if, as we were saying, opinion and knowledge are distinct faculties, then the sphere of knowledge and of opinion cannot be the same.

Then if being is the subject-matter of knowledge, something else must be the subject-matter of opinion?

Yes, something else.

Well, then, is not-being the subject-matter of opinion? Or rather, how can there be any opinion at all about not-being? Reflect: when a man has an opinion, has he not an opinion about something? Can he have an opinion which is an opinion about nothing?

Impossible . . . .

But were we not saying before that if anything appeared to be of a sort which both is and is not at the same time, that sort of thing would appear also to lie in the interval between pure being and absolute not-being; and that the corresponding faculty is neither knowledge nor ignorance, but will be found in the interval between them?

True.

And in that interval there has now been discovered something which we call opinion?

There has.

Then what remains to be discovered is the object which partakes equally of the nature of being and not-being, and cannot rightly be termed either, pure and simple. The unknown term, when discovered, we may truly call the subject of opinion . . .

True.

This being premised, I would ask the gentleman who is of the opinion that there is no absolute or unchangeable Idea of beauty—in whose opinion the beautiful (i.e., beauty itself) **is** (only) **in the manifold—he, I say,**

your lover of (many) **beautiful sights, who cannot bear to be told that the beautiful** (beauty itself) **is one, and the just is one, or that anything is one—to him I would appeal, saying: Will you be so very kind, sir, as to tell us whether, of all these beautiful things, there is one which will not be found** (to be also) **ugly; or of all the just things, one which will not be found unjust; or of the holy things, one which will not also be unholy?**

No, he replied; the beautiful will in some point of view be found ugly. And the same is true of the rest . . . .

Then those who see the many beautiful (things), **and who yet neither see absolute beauty nor can follow any guide who points the way thither; who see the many just** (things), **and not absolute justice, and the like—such persons may be said to have opinion but not knowledge?**

That is certain.

But those who see the absolute and eternal and immutable may be said to know, and not to have opinion only?

Neither can that be denied.

The one love and embrace the subjects of knowledge, the other those of opinion? The latter are the same, as I dare say you will remember, who listened to sweet sounds and gazed upon fair colors, but would not tolerate the existence of absolute beauty?

Yes, I remember.

Shall we then be guilty of any impropriety in calling them lovers of opinion rather than lovers of wisdom (philosophers)**? And will they be very angry with us for thus describing them?**

I shall tell them not to be angry; no man should be angry at what is true.

But those who love the truth in each thing are to be called lovers of wisdom and not lovers of opinion.

Assuredly.

And thus, Glaucon, after the argument has gone a weary way, the true and the false philosophers have at length appeared in view . . .

And what is the next question? He asked.

Surely, I said, the one which follows next in order. Inasmuch as philosophers only are able to grasp the eternal and unchangeable, and those who wander in the region of the many and variable are

not philosophers, I must ask you which of the two classes should be the rulers of our state?

Note the necessary connection between theory and practice, philosophy and politics, right and might, wisdom and power. This is Plato's prescription for a good society: put might into the hands of right, political power into the hands of the wise, rather than ascribing the name of right to whatever laws fools have the might to make (which is Thrasymachus' definition of justice). Fortify justice instead of justifying force.

But to do this very practical thing, we need to do a very theoretical thing: we need to know what wisdom is. To do ethics and politics aright we need to do metaphysics and epistemology.

And Plato's basic answer is that wisdom is the ability to judge what many particular concrete temporal things and persons and laws and practices are just by the standard of the knowledge of justice itself, which is one universal abstract eternal essence or nature or "Platonic Idea."

This is Plato's famous "Theory of Ideas." Be sure you capitalize the "I," for these Ideas are not subjective but objective, not invented but discovered. They don't come from our minds but *into* our minds. Not only must we judge particular laws and persons and acts by the standard of Ideas like Justice itself, but we must also judge *ideas* by such Ideas, judge *our* ideas by *the* Ideas, judge our opinions by objective truths.

But we can't do that if these Ideas don't exist. Thus ethics and politics depend on metaphysics. If there are no such things as Ideas, or eternal, unchangeable essences, we cannot ever find them. And they include not only the nature of justice but also the nature of man, the nature of ourselves. What is the human essence? That is what Socrates meant by his famous command (borrowed from the Delphic oracle) "Know thyself." He did not mean "know the facts about your unique individual psychological makeup" but "know the universal essence of humanity, and know the universal Good which is the ultimate end and purpose and goal of all our actions."

We can know what we ought to do, how we ought to live, both socially (politics) and individually (ethics) only if we know what we are, what kind of being we have—and that is metaphysics. Are we merely parts of nature or are we also, by our reason, creatures that are also supernatural, transcendent to nature, judges of nature?

"Nature" here includes the irrational passions that come to our reason and will as well as the physical things and sensations that come to us, as they come to the animals. This is the basic difference between philosophers like Bacon, Hobbes, Hume, Sartre, Nietzsche, and Russell, who are naturalists, and Plato, Aristotle, Augustine, Aquinas, Descartes, Leibnitz, Kant, and Kierkegaard, who are supernaturalists. "Supernaturalism" here does not necessarily mean the occult, miracles, mysticism, or religion. What transcends Nature for Plato is Reason (in the old, big sense) in us and the "Ideas" in objective reality.

If you agree with the metaphysics of Thrasymachus and the Sophists and the Naturalists, then you will also have to agree with their ethics. If there are no supernatural goods, no real moral absolutes that are universal and unchangeable, no "higher law" than particular and changeable man-made laws, then man cannot seek or find or know or live by them. And then Socrates is an unrealistic dreamer and Thrasymachus, even though he is a bit rough around the edges with his talk about power, is essentially right.

Plato in the *Republic* wants to expand our world (metaphysics) and our mind (epistemology) and our self-image (anthropology) and our destiny (ethics) as well as our society (politics). All of this is symbolized by the prisoners' escape from the "cave," the most famous image in the history of philosophy, which is coming up next, or almost next.

Plato does not deny that the changing world of nature is real and important and valuable and must be known. It is not an illusion. But it is an image of a higher, greater "world" or dimension or kind of reality. It is like a sign: it is real, but it points beyond itself to something else. It fitfully reflects this other kind of reality. White things reflect whiteness (but also non-whiteness; they are mixed). Dogs reflect dogginess, or the nature of dogs. Humans have humanity (but also inhumanity!). Just persons, laws, states, and acts have justice, reflect justice, reveal (but also partly conceal) justice as a photograph or a painting or a mirror image reveals (and may partly also conceal) a person or thing. The image is real, but the thing it is an image of is more real, real in a greater sense. The thing of which the images are images are the Ideas. We think of "ideas," with a small "I," as our mental images of material things; Plato thinks of material things as images of the Ideas with a capital I.

They are universals, or one-in-many (one essence in many particular things). They are unmixed and perfect. In the material world there's a little non-x in every x. And they are unchangeable. In the universe, everything is constantly changing. White houses soon become grey, but whiteness does not.

These Ideas are not just ideas, any more than they are things. Both things (kind of reality #1) and ideas (kind of reality #2, mental activities) change. Platonic Ideas (kind of reality #3) are timeless. They are not opinions in our minds, for they measure and judge our opinions. We have ideas and opinions about them, but they are not themselves ideas or opinions. They are realities, though not material or temporal realities.

If you balk at thinking of Ideas that are not in any minds at all, think of them as ideas in the mind of a perfect, eternal God. That is the essential addition St. Augustine made to Plato: he gave Plato's Ideas a home. Plato (who like Socrates was a monotheist) did not explicitly affirm that, but he did not deny it either.

Plato's simplest argument for the existence of the Ideas is our mental experience. As real material things impinge on our senses, the Ideas impinge on our minds. We discover, we do not create, the nature of a triangle and the laws of trigonometry. We create only the language systems to express these laws. And we create different languages, including different mathematical languages, but the truth they all express is one and the same. The same is true of ethics. Though of course ethical truths are not as easy to find, and not as cut and dried, as mathematics truths—they are just as objectively real.

If they are merely our own feelings, how can we argue about them? We don't argue about our personal tastes (in food, e.g.), unless we are very arrogant or stupid. I like chocolate, you like vanilla. That's all. But we argue about ethical goods and evils.

Furthermore, if ethical ideals are only man-made and subjective, why do they come to us with authority? Why are we bound in conscience to obey them? Why *must* we be fans of justice, though we can't say we *must* be fans of baseball? If we made the rules of ethics as we make the rules of baseball, we can also unmake them. But we can't unmake them, any more than we can unmake the laws of mathematics. Our mind bumps up against the unchangeable truth that the interior angles of a triangle must equal 180 degrees, and it also bumps up against the unchangeable truth that justice is a virtue and always is good ("profitable") for us.

As different physical roads necessarily lead us to different physical destinations (you can't walk to the Pacific Ocean by walking east from Chicago) and as different mathematical roads necessarily lead us to different mathematical destinations (you can't arrive at an odd number by adding up any number of even numbers), so different moral roads (justice and injustice) necessarily lead us to different moral destinations: wisdom vs. folly, virtue vs. vice, blessedness vs. misery, ultimately some kind of Heaven vs. Hell.

The ethical application of Plato's Theory of Ideas, the difference it makes, can hardly be exaggerated. This is the fundamental point of the *Republic,* and the fundamental difference between life in the cave and life outside it. It is the difference between two completely different, exactly opposite, philosophies of life; it is two opposite answers to the greatest of all questions: What is the good, the greatest good, the *summum bonum*, the end to which all other goods are means? What is the meaning of life? What is the purpose of my existence? What am I here for? What ought I to be and do?

If nature (the cave) is the only reality, then my end and my good and my duties must be limited to nature, to the kind of reality nature offers me: food, drink, sex, pleasure, riches, and (if I am altruistically and communally inclined) the friendship and admiration of my fellow men. If, on the other hand, I am in contact also with another kind of reality, which transcends nature, then my ethical life too comes from and refers to that: something timeless and unchangeable in its being and absolute in its goodness. Then the meaning of life will be for me to increase my knowledge of and conformity to this Idea of the Good, and to regulate my actions in this world by that knowledge. In other words, each of us must be a philosopher-king in his or her own life.

We live in a society (Western civilization) whose most radical philosophical departure from the past is not technology or democracy but the abandonment of this Platonic perspective, often called the idea of a natural moral law, a higher (eternal, unchangeable) law than any man-made (and therefore changeable) laws, in the name of which one can criticize and change man-made laws. (Only a traditionalist can be a principled revolutionary.)

I've taken a long time to make this one point of Plato's because this is not just one of his ideas, it's his one "big idea." And it divides our world today more radically than any other divide. The Sophists are still with us, especially in our philosophy departments and law schools. We are living in the first society in the history of the world the majority of whose intellectuals no longer believe in this essential Platonic point. You could call that point "the Theory of Ideas," or "moral absolutism," or "objective values," or "a natural moral law," or Tao, or Rta, or Logos—different cultures have different terms for it. But it is, for a Platonist, the essential definition of civilization. (Aristotle does not fundamentally disagree with Plato here, he merely tweaks him, though it is a big tweak. He disagrees not with the *existence* of the Ideas, only with their "separation" from material things. Aristotle agrees that unchangeable Platonic Ideas exist—he calls them "forms"—but he says they exist in things, joined to things, together with matter rather than separated from matter, in a hylomorphic (matter-and-form) unity.)

Would Plato say that we are no longer living in civilization once we cease to believe in the Ideas, especially in ethics? To answer that question for yourself, read Huxley's "Brave New World." It is a prophetic picture of our society in the near future. The only truly civilized person there is called "the Savage." He is not a typical American; he is a Native American.

8. Plato's Parables of the Sun, the Line, and the Cave

Plato then proceeds to give us three concrete pictures, myths, allegories, analogies, or parables that stick in our mind much more readily than abstract arguments. They all point to the supreme reality, the supreme Idea, which he calls simply "The Good" (or Goodness Itself). It is "the big Idea."

Glaucon praises Socrates for having defined Justice, and asks him whether he can similarly define Goodness, of which justice is only one part or instance. Socrates replies that he cannot, because definitions are, by definition, finite ("de-fino" means "to put limits around") while the supreme Good is infinite. But even though he can't get there to measure and define it, he can offer three approaches to it from a distance, so to speak: three analogies or likenesses.

The Sun

The first is the sun. As the sun is the single source of all (natural) light in the world the objects of understanding (the Ideas or Forms like Justice).

Just as we can't look at the sun itself without going blind, and yet without the sun and its light we could see nothing, so we can't rationally define the Absolute Good itself (it is very like the God of theism that way, though Plato does not say it is a Person) and yet without it and its giving meaning and intelligibility to the world of Ideas, we could not understand anything in that world. Let one thing be mystical and indefinable, and everything else becomes rational and definable.

The Divided Line

Plato then gives us a second image, which is a hierarchy or ladder to climb. There are four steps on this ladder or stairway. He tells us to imagine a line divided into four parts, each part larger than the one below it. (Different sizes or lengths here symbolize different degrees of rationality or intelligibility.) These will be the four steps of our exit from the cave, and also the four steps in Plato's educational system. They are the four levels of knowing, so they are a summary of Plato's epistemology. But they are also four levels of being or reality known or knowable, so they are also a summary of Plato's metaphysics.

The first is the sensing of images of physical things: reflections in mirrors or in the water, or pictures or artistic representations of things. Being only images, they are less real than the things of which they are images.

The second is direct sensation of real physical things.

The third is the understanding of mathematical Ideas, quantitative Forms, like triangles or numbers. This uses not sensation but logical, deductive reasoning, as in algebra or geometry.

The fourth is the vision of the Ideas, the qualitative Forms like Justice. This is neither sensation nor calculative reasoning but intellectual intuition, contemplation, understanding. It is the highest meaning of Reason for Plato.

The Good is not on the line, but off of it, or on top of it, or beyond it. The line does not give us the Good but gives is the direction towards it.

The Line thus gives us four levels of knowing and four corresponding levels of being, or reality. It is a set of categories that can prove to be an extremely useful device for classifying any philosopher's metaphysics or epistemology.

The Cave

And now, I said, let me show in a figure how far our nature is enlightened and unenlightened.

Behold! Human beings living in an underground den, which has a mouth open towards the light and reaching all along the den.

Here they have been from their childhood, and they have their legs and necks chained so that they cannot move, and can only see before them, being prevented by the chains from turning round their heads.

Above them and behind them a fire is blazing at a distance, and between the fire and the prisoners there is a raised way, and you will see, if you look, a low wall build along the way, like the screen which marionette players have in front of them, over which they show the puppets.

I see.

And do you see, I said, men passing along the wall carrying all sorts of vessels and statues and figures of animals made of wood and stone and various materials, which appear over the wall? Some of them are talking, others silent.

You have shown me a strange image, and they are strange prisoners.

Like ourselves! I replied. And they see only their own shadows, or the shadows of one another, which the fire throws on the opposite wall of the cave.

True, he said. How could they see anything but the shadows if they were never allowed to move their heads?

And of the objects which are being carried in like manner they would only see the shadows.

Yes, he said.

And if they were able to converse with one another, would they not suppose that they were naming what was actually before them?

Very true.

And suppose further that the prison had an echo which came from the other side. Would they not be sure to fancy when one of the passers-by spoke that the voice which they heard came from the passing shadow?

No question, he replied.

To them, I said, the truth would be literally nothing but the shadows of the images.

That is certain.

And now look again, and see what will naturally follow if the prisoners are released and disabused of their error. At first, when any of them is liberated and compelled suddenly to stand up and turn his neck round and walk and look towards the light, he will suffer sharp pains. The glare will distress him, and he will be unable to see the realities of which in his former state he had seen the shadows.

And then conceive someone saying to him that what he saw before was an illusion, but that now, when he is approaching nearer to being and his eye is turned towards more real existence, he has a clearer vision—what will be his reply? And you may further imagine

that his instructor is pointing to the objects as they pass and requiring him to name them—will he not be perplexed? Will he not fancy that the shadows which he formerly saw are truer than the objects which are now shown to him?

Far truer.

And if he is compelled to look straight at the light, will he not have a pain in his eyes which will make him turn away to take refuge in the objects of vision which he can see, and which he will conceive to be in reality clearer than the things which are now being shown to him?

True, he said.

And suppose once more that he is reluctantly dragged up a steep and rugged ascent, and held fast until he is forced into the presence of the sun himself. Is he not likely to be pained and irritated? When he approaches the light, his eyes will be dazzled, and he will not be able to see anything at all of what are now called realities.

Not all in a moment, he said.

He will require to grow accustomed to the sight of the upper world. And first he will see the shadows best, next the reflections of men and other objects in the water, and then the objects themselves. Then he will gaze upon the light of the moon and the stars and the spangled heaven. And he will see the sky and the stars by night better than the sun or the light of the sun by day.

Certainly.

Last of all he will be able to see the sun, and not mere reflections of him in the water, but he will see him in his own proper place and not in another, and he will contemplate him as he is.

Certainly.

He will then proceed to argue that this is he who gives the seasons and years, and is the guardian of all that is in the visible world, and in a certain way is the cause of all things which he and his fellows have been accustomed to behold.

Clearly, he said, he would first see the sun and then reason about him.

And when he remembered his old habitation, and the wisdom of the den and his fellow-prisoners, do you not suppose that he would felicitate (congratulate) **himself on the change, and pity them?**

Certainly he would.

And if they were in the habit of conferring honors among themselves on those who were quickest to observe the passing shadows and to tell which of them went before, and which followed after, and which were together, do you think that he would care for such honors and glories, or envy the possessors of them? Would he not say with Homer, "Better to be the poor servant of a poor master" and to endure anything, rather than think as they do and live after their manner?

Yes, he said, I think that he would rather suffer anything than entertain those false notions and live in this miserable manner.

Imagine once more, I said, such a one coming suddenly out of the sun to be replaced into his old situation. Would he not be certain to have his eyes full of darkness?

To be sure, he said.

And if there were a contest, and he had to compete in measuring the shadows with the prisoners who had never moved out of the den, while his sight was still weak, and before his eyes had become steady—and the time which would be needed to acquire this new habit of sight might be very considerable—would he not be ridiculous? Men would say of him that up he went and down he came without his eyes; and that it was better not even to think of ascending. And if anyone tried to loose another and lead him up to the light, let them only catch the offender and they would put him to death.

No question, he said.

This entire allegory, I said, you may now add, dear Glaucon, to the previous argument. The prison-house is the world of sight. The light of the fire is the sun. And you will not misapprehend me if you interpret the journey upwards to be the ascent of the soul into the intellectual world, according to my poor opinion, which at your desire I have expressed, whether rightly or wrongly, God knows.

But whether true or false, my opinion is that in the world of knowledge the Idea of Good appears last of all, and is seen only with an effort, and when seen it is also inferred to be the universal author of all things beautiful and right, the parent of light and the lord of light in this visible world, and the immediate source of truth in the

intellectual world. And this is the power upon which he must have his eye fixed who would act rationally either in public or private life.

I agree, he said, as far as I am able to understand you.

Moreover, I said, you must not wonder that those who attain to this beatific vision are unwilling to descend to human affairs. For their souls are ever hastening into the upper world where they desire to dwell, which desire of theirs is very natural, if our allegory may be trusted.

Yes, very natural.

And is there anything surprising in one who passes from divine contemplations to the evil state of man misbehaving himself in a ridiculous manner, if, while his eyes are blinking and before he has become accustomed to the surrounding darkness, he is compelled to fight in courts of law, or in other places, about the images or the shadows of images of justice, and is endeavoring to meet the conceptions of those who have never yet seen absolute justice?

Anything but surprising, he replied.

Anyone who has common sense will remember that the bewilderments of the eyes are of two kinds, and arise from two causes: either from coming out of the light or from going into the light—which is true of the mind's eye quite as much as of the bodily eye. And he who remembers this when he sees anyone whose vision is perplexed and weak, will not be too ready to laugh. He will first ask whether the soul of that man has come out of the brighter life, and is unable to see because he is unaccustomed to the dark, or having turned from darkness to the day is dazzled by excess of light. And he will count one happy in his condition and state of being, and he will pity the other. Or, if he have a mind to laugh at the soul which comes from below into the light, there will be more reason in this than in the laugh which greets him who returns from above out of the light into the den.

That, he said, is a very just distinction.

But then, if I am right, certain professors of education must be wrong when they say that they can put a knowledge into the soul which was not there before, like sight into blind eyes.

They undoubtedly say this, he replied.

But our argument shows that the power and capacity of learning exists in the soul already, and that just as the eye was unable to turn from darkness to light without the whole body (turning), so too the instrument of knowledge can only by the movements of the whole soul be turned from the world of becoming to the world of being, and learn by degrees to endure the sight of being, and of the brightest and best of being, in other words, of The Good.

Very true.

Commentary on this classic passage would be like snow on a bell. Let it ring its Platonic music without muffling it with mushy modern comments.

9. Education and Politics; The Parallel Between Souls and States

And must there not be some art which will effect conversion in the easiest and quickest manner, not implanting the faculty of sight, for that exists already, but has been turned in the wrong direction, and is looking away from the truth?

This "art" is, of course, education, which Plato points to as the single most important institution in human life and the most crucial causal difference between good and bad states and souls. Plato will lay the foundations for "liberal arts education" in Book 7, which defines the essential curriculum which will prevail for more than two millennia in the university, that invention of Plato's (his "academy" was the world's first university, from which the very term "academic" is derived) which has dominated Western civilization more than any other institution ever invented by man. Even the Italian Communist philosopher Gramsci understood this, and wrote that Communism will never win the world on the battlefield or the ballot box but only in the classroom. The "cave" is not just politics but education. The cave is the classroom, or the mind of the student.

Platonism has proved itself almost as remarkably unworkable in politics as it has proved itself workable in individual lives. Plato's psychology and individual ethics is one of the great achievements of human thought; Plato's politics is almost one of its greatest jokes. The *Republic* began with the line "I went down to the Piraeus," i.e., to politics, from Athens, i.e., from philosophy. And here, at the center of the *Republic*, we find the true philosopher going back down into the cave (of politics) to liberate its prisoners. The trip up has inspired many; the trip down has largely been disastrous. The most quoted saying of William F. Buckley reflects this judgment: "I'd rather be governed by the first 2,000 names in the Boston telephone directory than by the faculty of Harvard." Democracy, which Plato scorned, has proved itself more lasting and successful than elitism, which he loved, in the state.

But not in the soul. The equality of all ideas and values in the soul, as distinct from the equality of all citizens in the state, has proved to be simply catastrophic and destructive. An aristocracy in the soul (i.e., the rule of reason, an interior hierarchy, judging lesser ideas and values by higher ones, judging actions by ideas (principles) and values, and judging feelings and passions by reason), seems even more universally necessary in souls than democracy in states. So Plato's assumption that souls and states are mirror images of each other seems to have been massively disproved in human history. We read Plato today for his psychology, not his politics.

And yet his critique of democracy in Book 8 remains a test, a touchstone. If we cannot answer it, then Plato refutes democracy rather than democracy refuting Plato. And it is a serious critique, putting into question the very thing we take for granted as unquestionably good, viz. freedom.

In both souls and states, Plato's prescription for justice and happiness is the rule of reason, which for him means not cleverness but wisdom. Philosophy, by definition, means the love of wisdom. This is why "philosophers must become kings or kings become philosophers": so that wisdom and power are joined, and instead of pinning the label of "right" onto political might, political might may be given to true right, and justice be fortified instead of force being justified. This is Plato's solution to the problem of evil and injustice both for souls and for states.

And this is why Plato insists that philosophers must be compelled to rule rather than voted into office: because is it mainly fools who vote and only fools (or saints) who voluntarily run for office:

Then, I said, the business of us who are the founders of the state will be to compel the best minds to attain that knowledge which we have already shown to be the greatest of all—they must continue to ascend until they arrive at the Good; but when they have ascended and seen enough, we must not allow them to do as they do now.

What do you mean?

I mean that they remain in the upper world. But this must not be allowed. They must be made to descend again among the prisoners in the den, and partake of their labors and honors, whether they are worth having or not.

But is not this unjust? he said. Ought we to give them a worse life when they might have a better?

You have again forgotten, my friend, I said, the intention of the legislator, who did not aim at making any one class in the state happy above the rest. The happiness was to be in the whole state . . . . Wherefore each of you, when his turn comes, must go down to the general underground abode, and get the habit of seeing in the dark. When you have acquired the habit, you will see ten thousand times better than the inhabitants of the den, and you will know what the several images are and what they represent, because you have seen the beautiful and just and good in their truth.

And thus our state, which is yours also, will be a reality, and not a dream only, and will be administered in a spirit unlike that of other states, in which men fight with one another about shadows only, and are distracted in the struggle for power, which in their eyes is a great good. Whereas the truth is that the state in which the rulers are most reluctant to govern is always the best and most quietly governed, and the state in which they are most eager, the worst . . . . And the only life which looks down upon the life of political ambition is that of true philosophy. (520-1)

Plato here appeals to what C. S. Lewis calls the principle of "first and second things": only when first things are put first are second things attained too. When second things (like power, and politics) are put first and first things (like wisdom, and philosophy, which is the love of wisdom) are put second, the second things as well as the first things are perverted and lost. Thus the absolutizers and idolaters of politics always pervert it, while those who put it second are the only ones who can perfect it. How ironic that most modern minds read the *Republic* itself as primarily about politics! By this they prove that they have failed to learn its primary lesson.

10. The Seven Liberal Arts: Plato's Curriculum

In Plato's view, the goodness and happiness of the state depends on the wisdom of its rulers, and this, in turn, depends on their proper education. Therefore, Plato says, the single most important institution in the state is education. Book 7 describes this education, which will bring new philosophers-to-be out of the cave and fit them to rule. However, that practical payoff is not its only purpose: it exists also simply to know the truth for its own sake, which is the essential meaning of the concept of "liberal education." That concept has largely become lost in our culture, or even denied, by skeptics and subjectivists who say there is no such thing as "objective truth," at least where values are concerned.

Book 7 became the basic curricular design for university education for the next 2000 years. The medieval term for it was "the seven liberal arts." They were called "liberal" arts because they "liberated" the mind from the cave of ignorance (not just factual ignorance but philosophical ignorance), and because these subjects, or the study of these subjects, were like freemen, existing for their own sake rather than for the sake of their masters, like slaves. (The ancients regarded "practical" or "professional" studies such as economics as inferior in value for this reason: they were "slavish" in that they sought truth not for itself but as a means or practical instrument for some other end, as a slave, according to his master, exists only for his master rather than for himself.)

Plato's educational scheme began with two preliminary subjects in early childhood: music and gymnastic (exercise), which introduced harmony into the emotions and into the body, as a farmer would introduce fertilizer into the soil, so that when he seeded the soil, better and healthier plants would grow. The farmer is the teacher, the soil is the sub-rational dimensions of his student, and the plant is rational justice, the master virtue. Justice is a kind of harmony (thus its close resemblance to music): it is the harmony of the soul. For Plato, as for Confucius, harmony is the very essential structure of justice: each power of the soul and each class of the state doing its natural work with its natural virtue.

These two social reformers had similar ideas but dissimilar results. Plato's attempt to institute his "republic" in Syracuse, Sicily, at the invitation of his cousin Dionysus, its ruler, was not a success—in fact, Plato barely escaped with his life. But Confucius was the most successful social reformer in history. His teachings "took" in China for 2000 years after his death, and held together the world's most populous nation longer than any other, mainly because of its focus on social harmony. Musical harmony, for Plato, was a precursor of that, and therefore crucial to the beginning of education.

After music and gymnastics comes what we call the arts and sciences. First the sciences. They come first because they are easier to grasp than the more philosophical "arts" because they are more clear and concrete, less abstract—although all these subjects, being subjects of reason, demand some degree of abstraction.

They are four because they correspond to the four dimensions of the concrete physical universe: arithmetic (one-dimensional reality), plane geometry (two-dimensional reality), solid geometry (three-dimensional reality), and physics, or astronomy, or cosmology (four-dimensional reality, including the changes through time of three-dimensional bodies). The Greeks used knotted cords or pebbles placed along lines in the sand to do their arithmetical and geometrical calculations; thus the word "calculus" is the Greek word for "pebble."

The last three subjects to be tanght are grammar, rhetoric, and dialectic. "Grammar" means the structure and rules of language itself. "Rhetoric" means not emotional tricks to blind the reason, but simply effective writing and speaking. "Dialectic" means logic, the art of argument, which Plato learned from Socrates' practice and which Plato's disciple, Aristotle, first codified in the world's first logic textbook, the "Organon," or "instrument." (It was logic as a human instrument using ordinary language and common sense rather than the mathematical, impersonal computer logic that is in fashion today.)

Instead of feeding the mind the facts about the world, these three arts train the mind itself, and its expression in language. This is why

Dorothy Sayers calls for the restoration of these "lost tools of learning," in a famous essay by that title which is a kind of charter or credo for most classical education programs today.

To put all this into the context of Plato's "big picture," these seven (really nine) subjects are steps on the ladder of learning, steps on the "divided line," steps in the journey out of the cave. Education, like life, is a journey, with an end. And the end is the highest wisdom, which is the understanding of the Idea of The Good, or the Essence of Goodness Itself.

This is to Plato what God is to theists. It may be regarded as the divine nature without any known Person to have it. This is why, though Plato was not a personal theist, personal theists (Jews, Christians and Muslims) usually have much less difficulty understanding Plato than atheists do.

11. Book 8: Four Kinds of Unjust States: Plato's Critique of Democracy

The just state, according to Plato, is the one ruled by the best people. That is the meaning of "aristocracy"—"aristos" means "the best" or "excellence," and cracy" means "rule." "Demos" means "the people" or "the masses." Thus aristocracy means rule by the best and democracy means rule by everyone.

An aristocracy, according to Plato's theory of history, naturally degenerates into a timocracy, or the rule of the brave, when the military class rebels against the philosopher-kings. This class still has a sense of honor and courage, but lacks wisdom.

This, in turn, degenerates into a plutocracy when the rich producers seize power. They lack both wisdom and courage but they still have self-control, self-discipline, temperance, or moderation, for they believe in delayed gratification and put the necessary desires before the unnecessary, or luxurious ones.

The next step in degeneration is democracy, when the masses rule, and devote themselves to luxuries, or unnecessary desires. Plato's critique of democracy (the boldface type section below) is a challenging thought experiment for us, who almost always defend it.

The final step in degeneration is tyranny, which comes about from the lack of order in the masses and their devotion to luxuries. Democracy is close to anarchy, and the need for order is met by the tyrant, the man on the white horse, the "savior."

In the next book (9) Plato traces a similar four-fold degeneration in the aristocratic soul, or individual. The philosopher-king's son sees his father as less exciting and less courageous than a soldier, because he has let the spirited part rule in his soul rather than reason. The soldier's son, in turn, prefers to pursue wealth rather than honor like his father, and becomes a disciplined and successful money-maker. His son, in turn, inheriting his father's wealth without effort, has no discipline and squanders it, devoting himself to not just the necessary desire\s, like his father, but to the unnecessary desires, i.e., to luxuries. Finally, the son of the luxurious man becomes addicted to a single desire, the desire for power, and becomes a tyrant. The tyrant successfully persuades the masses because they no longer live by the wisdom of the deposed philosopher-kings, or the honor of the soldiers, or even the self-discipline of the plutocrats.

These two devolutionary scripts are sometimes lived out in the lives of states and/or of families, but Plato seems to present them as natural and inevitable. History has proved that they are not.

But Plato's main point here is not a factually accurate history of particular states or families, but a universal definition of injustice so that we can compare it to justice and finally decide the single main question of the *Republic*, which way is the more profitable way to live? Justice comes in one form, injustice in four. And once we understand both justice and injustice, we shall find little or no more argument necessary.

What follows is Plato's critique of democracy. Find what you think are the truths in it and find also what you think are Plato's errors and refute them.

And now what is their manner of life, and what sort of a government have they? For as the government is, such will be the man.

Clearly, he said.

In the first place, are they not free? And is not the city full of freedom and frankness? A man may say and do what he likes.

'Tis said so, he replied.

And where freedom is, the individual is clearly able to order for himself his own life as he pleases?

Clearly.

Then in this kind of state there will be the greatest variety of human natures?

There will.

This, then, seems likely to be the fairest of states, being like an embroidered robe which is spangled with every sort of flower. And just as women and children think a variety of colors to be of all things most charming, so there are many men to whom this state, which is spangled with the manners and characters of mankind, will appear to be the fairest of states.

Yes.

Yes, my good sir, and there will be no better in which to look for a government.

Why?

Because of the liberty which reigns there. They have a complete assortment of constitutions. And he who has a mind to establish a state, as we have been doing, must go to a democracy as he would to a bazaar at which they sell them, and pick out the one that suits him. Then, when he has made his choice, he may found his state.

He will be sure to have patterns enough.

And there being no necessity, I said, for you to govern in this state, even if you have the capacity, or to be governed, unless you like, or to go to war when the rest go to war, or to be at peace when others are at peace, unless you are so disposed . . . is not this a way of life which for the moment is supremely delightful?

For the moment, yes.

. . . These and other kindred characteristics are proper to democracy, which is a charming form of government, full of variety and disorder, and dispensing a sort of equality to equals and unequals alike.

We know her well.

Consider now, I said, what manner of man the individual is, or . . . how he comes into being . . . . the young man passes out of his

original nature, which was trained in the school of necessity, into the freedom and libertinism of useless and unnecessary pleasures . . . After this he lives on, spending his money and labor and time on unnecessary pleasures quite as much as on necessary ones . . .

Very true, he said.

Neither does he receive . . . any true word of advice. If anyone says to him that some pleasures are the satisfactions of good and noble desires, and others of evil desires, and that he ought to use and honor some and chastise and master the others—whenever this is repeated to him he shakes his head and says that they are all alike, and that one is as good as another.

Yes, he said, that is the way with him.

Yes, I said, he lives from day to day indulging the appetite of the hour. And sometimes he is lapped in drink and strains of the flute. Then he becomes a water drinker and tries to get thin. Then he takes a turn at gymnastics, sometimes idling and neglecting everything, then once more living the life of a philosopher. Often he is busy with politics, and starts to his feet and says and does whatever comes into his head. And if he is emulous of anyone who is a warrior, off he is in that direction. Or of men of business, once more in that. His life has neither law nor order. And this distracted existence he terms joy and bliss and freedom. And so he goes on.

Yes, he replied, he is all liberty and equality.

Yes, I said, his life is motley and manifold and an epitome of the lives of many. He matches the state which we described as fair and spangled . . . .

We say of power that "all power tends to corrupt, and absolute power corrupts absolutely." Thus Gyges' (and Gollum's) Ring is extremely dangerous. Why do we not say the same thing about freedom?

12. The Main Point Finally Proved: The Profit (Happiness) in Justice

Well, I said, now having arrived at this state of the argument, we may revert to the words which brought us hither. Was not someone

saying that injustice was a gain to the perfectly unjust man who was reputed to be just?

Yes, that was said.

Now then, having determined the power and quality of justice, let us have a little conversation with him.

What shall we say to him?

Let us make an image of the soul (of this successful tyrant), **that he may have his own words presented before his eyes** (so that he may understand what he is saying).

Of what sort?

An ideal image of the soul, like the composite creations of ancient mythology, such as the Chimera or Scylla or Cerberus. And there are many others in which two or more different natures are said to grow into one.

There are said to have been such unions.

Then do you now model the form of the multitudinous, many-headed monster, having a ring of heads of all manner of beasts, tame and wild, which he is able to generate and metamorphose at will.

You suppose marvelous powers in the artist. But, as language is more pliable than wax or any similar substance, let there be such a model as you propose.

Suppose now that you make a second form, as of a lion; and a third, of a man—the second smaller than the first and the third smaller than the second.

That is an easier task, he said; and I have made them as you say.

And now join them, and let the three grow into one.

That has been accomplished.

Next, fashion the outside of them into a single image, as of a man, so that he who is not able to look within, and sees only the outer hull, may believe the beast to be a single human creature.

I have done so, he said.

And now, to him who maintains that it is profitable for the human creature to be unjust, and unprofitable to be just, let us reply that, if he be right, it is profitable for this creature to feast the multitudinous monster and strengthen the lion and the lion-like qualities, but to starve and weaken the man, who is consequently liable

to be dragged about at the mercy of either of the other two. And he is not to attempt to familiarize or harmonize them with one another. He ought rather to suffer them to fight and bite and devour one another.

Certainly, he said. That is what the approver of injustice says.

To him, the supporter of justice makes answer that he should ever so speak and act as to give the man within him in some way or other the most complete mastery over the entire human creature. He should watch over the many-headed monster like a good husbandman, fostering and cultivating the gentle qualities, and preventing the wild ones from growing. He should be making the lion-heart his ally. And, in common care of them all, should be uniting the several parts with one another and with himself.

Yes, he said. That is quite what the maintainer of justice would say . . . .

Then how would a man profit if he received gold and silver on the condition that he was to enslave the noblest part of him to the worst? Who can imagine that a man who sold his son or daughter into slavery for money, especially if he sold them into the hands of fierce and evil men, would be the gainer, however large might be the sum he received? And will anyone say that he is not miserable who remorselessly sells his own divine (godlike) **being to that which is most godless and detestable? . . . From what point of view, then, and on what ground can we say that a man is profited by injustice or intemperance or other baseness, which will make him a worse man, even though he acquire money or power by his wickedness?**

From no point of view at all.

What shall he profit, if his injustice be undetected and unpunished? He who is undetected only gets worse, whereas he who is detected and punished has the brutal part of his nature silenced and humanized. The gentler element in him is liberated, and his whole soul is perfected and ennobled . . .

Even the best logical arguments in the world proved insufficient to adequately prove Plato's main point in Book I. Socrates himself said he was dissatisfied, though Thrasymachus was refuted, because they still did not know the Form, the Idea, the essence of what they were talking about, Justice and Injustice. But the new and harder task, that of understanding the Platonic Ideas of Justice and Injustice, which took eight more books, has finally proved successful. The *Republic* has climbed its own "divided line" from opinions (Cephalus) to beliefs (Polemarchus) to logical reasoning (the dialog with Thrasymachus) to understanding the Ideas of Justice and Injustice in such a way that the truth forces itself upon our minds like the light of the noonday sun. It has shown itself to be one of the examples of "what we can't not know" (in the words of the title of a book by Jay Budziszewski). Our task is finished, except for an incomparably important postscript.

13. Life After Death: The Rest of the Story

At the beginning of Book 2, when Glaucon challenged Socrates to prove that justice is worth having for its own sake rather than merely for the rewards people give to it, Plato deliberately put aside the issue of heavenly, after-death rewards and punishments from the gods, so that he could prove that justice, by its own nature, always and everywhere, even in this life, is "profitable." Now that that has been proved, he adds the point that there is an even greater payoff in the next life. In other words Plato did the same kind of thing God did in the Bible, not clearly revealing the next life until His students, the people He chose to be His collective prophet to the world, had learned the first lesson, that the first reason to be good was simply to conform to the nature of ultimate reality, or God: "You must be holy because I the Lord am holy." Once this lesson is learned, we can safely learn about the greater rewards of the next life without it being a bribe that corrupts our motive.

Plato's argument here is not designed to prove that life after death is just, but to prove that it exists. That is the controversial question. Almost no one believes that there is an afterlife but it is not just: that God or the gods are waiting to sneer at you and abuse you; that injustice triumphs over justice in the end. In fact, one of the most popular arguments for the existence of Heaven is based on just the opposite as a premise: that since final justice must be done, and since it is not done on earth, there must be a next life where it is done. Plato does not use this argument because he believes that justice is done even in this life: that it is always "profitable" even if, as with Socrates, it is rewarded by foolish men with the payment of martyrdom.

Here is Plato's argument for life after death, or the immortality of the soul. (There are more arguments in the *Phaedo*, a whole long dialog about death and the death of Socrates. Its arguments are not as convincing (to me, anyway) as this one; but its final scene, of Socrates' death, is one of the most moving and famous in world literature, and is itself a kind of proof. For when the idea of death and the idea of Socrates thus meet, it is the idea of death that is changed, not the idea of Socrates. No one should be allowed to die without having read that scene.)

Yes, he said, I have been convinced by the argument, as I believe that anyone else would have been.

And yet no mention has been made of the greatest prizes and rewards which await virtue.

What? Are there any greater still? If there are, they must be of an inconceivable greatness.

Why, I said, what was ever great in a short time? The whole period of three score years and ten is surely but a little thing in comparison with eternity.

Say rather "nothing," he replied.

And should an immortal being seriously think of this little space rather than of the whole?

Of the whole, certainly. But why do you ask?

Are you not aware, I said, that the soul of man is immortal and imperishable?

He looked at me in astonishment, and said: No, by heaven! And are you really prepared to maintain this?

Yes, I said, I ought to be, and you too. There is no difficulty in proving it.

I see a great difficulty, but I should like to hear you state this argument of which you make so light.

Listen then.

I am attending.

There is a thing which you call "good" and another which you call "evil"?

Yes, he replied.

Would you agree with me in thinking that the corrupting and destroying element is the evil, and the saving and improving element the good?

Yes.

And you admit that every thing has a good and also an evil? As ophthalmia is the evil of the eyes, and disease of the whole body, as mildew is of corn, and rot of timber, or rust of copper and iron? In everything, or in almost everything, there is an inherent evil and disease?

Yes, he said.

And anything which is infected by any of these evils is made evil, and at last wholly dissolves and dies?

True.

The vice and evil which is inherent in each is the destruction of each; and if this does not destroy them, there is nothing else that will. For good certainly will not destroy them, nor that which is neither good nor evil.

Certainly not.

If, then, we find any nature which, having this inherent corruption, cannot be dissolved and destroyed (by it), **we may be certain that of such a nature there is no destruction.**

That may be assumed.

Well, I said, is there no evil which corrupts the soul?

Yes, he said; there are all the evils which we were just now passing in review: injustice, intemperance, cowardice, ignorance (the four cardinal vices, opposite the four cardinal virtues).

But does any of these dissolve or destroy her (the soul)**? And here do not let us fall into the error of supposing that the unjust and foolish man, when he is detected,** ***perishes*** **through his own injustice, which is an evil of the soul. Take the analogy of the body: The evil of the body is a disease which wastes and reduces and annihilates the body, and all the things of which we were just now speaking come to annihilation through their own corruption attaching to them and inhering in them and so destroying them. Is this not true?**

Yes.

Consider the soul in like manner. Does the injustice or other evil which exists in the soul waste and consume her? Do they by attaching to the soul and inhering in her at last bring her to death, and so separate her from the body?

Certainly not.

And yet, I said, it is unreasonable to suppose that anything can perish from without, through affection of external evil, which could not be destroyed from within by a corruption of its own.

It is, he replied . . . .

But the soul, which cannot be destroyed by any evil, whether inherent or external, must exist forever, and if existing forever, must be immortal.

Certainly . . . .

Then this must be our notion of the just man: that even when he is in poverty or sickness, or any other seeming misfortune, all things will in the end work together for good to him, in life and death. For the gods have a care of anyone whose desire is to become just and to be like God, as far as any man can attain the divine likeness, by the pursuit of virtue.

Yes, he said; if he is like God, he will surely not be neglected by Him.

This is the existential conclusion, or "bottom line," of the *Republic*. It is not a dispensable afterthought, a mere personal postscript. It is life-changing. It is "the meaning of life." If it is not true, it is at least the world's most interesting lie, far more dramatic and challenging than all the smelly little typically modern reductionisms that have shaped and skinnied down our souls.

III. 31 Footnotes to Plato: The Rest of the History of Philosophy

Alfred North Whitehead famously said that "the safest characterization of the history of Western philosophy is that it is a series of footnotes to Plato." Here are 31 footnotes to prove his point: that all other systems of philosophy after Plato are alternatives to Plato, corrections to Plato, additions to Plato, or subtractions from Plato.

What follows are 31 laughably inadequate oversimplifications if they are regarded as a history of Western philosophy. But it is a useful set of appetizers and samples for rank beginners, to show that Whitehead was right.

The Sophists were Plato's major opponents and critics, as they were to Socrates. But we cannot call them "footnotes to Plato" because they came before him rather than after him, and because he was a correction of them rather than they being a corrective to him. Nevertheless, they are the fundamental alternative to Plato in all times, including contemporary times. Though the Sophists were skeptics, they were skeptics because they taught that no one ever knew truth, but because they taught that no one ever was in error. Truth was not too high and holy and far away to reach, but too low and ordinary and present to miss. Truth was whatever you thought: "truth" could only be "your truth" or "my truth" rather than "Truth." Stephen Colbert calls this "truthiness." And since they were subjectivists and relativists about truth, they were also subjectivists and relativists about moral truth, or goodness, or virtue. The most famous saying of the most famous Sophist, Protagoras, was: "The individual man is the measure of all things," especially of truth and goodness. This old pre-Socratic philosophy is also the most up-to-date and contemporary and popular one today in the civization (ours!) that was founded by the Greeks. It was the philosophy of modern media and pop psychology.

1. Aristotle: Realism (Macedonian, 4th century B.C.)

Aristotle is the single most important, popular, and commonsensical corrective to Plato. Aristotle was Plato's most brilliant student. He founded the second university in history, the Lyceum, as the first major alternative to Plato's Academy. But he admired Plato so much that he did not do this until after Plato's death, and explained his "rebellion" apologetically: "Dear is Plato but dearer still is truth."

Aristotle is the master of common sense. The Middle Ages called him simply "The Philosopher." On every issue he takes a reasonable, middle-of-the-road position. His critics sometimes call him "excessively moderate," "extremely anti-extremist," or "fanatically non-fanatical." Where Plato comes to a point, Aristotle is well-rounded. (I refer to their minds, not their bodies. Plato was never called "Pinhead," nor Aristotle "Fatso.")

Aristotle modified Plato at the very heart and center of his philosophy: the Theory of Forms. And this had natural and necessary consequences in every other area, especially in anthropology, epistemology, ethics, and politics.

In metaphysics, Aristotle accepts the existence of the Forms—indeed, "form" is the most basic concept in his entire philosophy—but he denies the "separation," or separate existence, of the Forms. He says that these universal natures or qualities or essences exist only in particular material things, and then in the particular human minds that abstract them mentally from things. Treeness is only in trees, and in our concept of trees. If all trees died, and all men stopped thinking of them, there would be no more treeness. But there would be according to Plato.

Aristotle's anthropology follows his metaphysics. As forms exist only in and with matter, according to Aristotle, so human souls exist only in and with human bodies. Where Plato said we are composed of two different things or entities or beings or substances, mind and matter (that was the premise of his proof for immortality at the end of the *Republic*), Aristotle says we are a single "substance" or entity of which our soul (mind) and our body are the two metaphysical dimensions, the form and the matter, like the meaning and the words of a book. On the one hand, Plato justifies the soul's separate immortality; Aristotle seems to deny it, and to reduce us to this-world-only creatures. On the other hand, Aristotle justifies our psychosomatic unity; Plato seems to deny it, and reduce us to houses (bodies) haunted by ghosts (souls). It took the genius of Aquinas, 1300 years later, to reconcile these two desirable ideas (immortality and psychon somatic unity).

Aristotle's epistemology (theory of knowledge) follows his metaphysics, as does Plato's. Whereas Plato is a Rationalist, who believed in the power of reason to know truth independent of the body's senses (by "recollection" of what was later called "innate ideas," ideas of the Ideas), Aristotle is a "soft" Empiricist (or sense-experience-ist) who believed that knowledge always begins in sense experience, though it does not end there and is not limited to sense experience, as "hard" Empiricism claims. And this difference in epistemology depends on their difference in metaphysics: If the Forms exist separate from matter, reason can know them separate from sensation, but if forms exist only in matter, then reason must abstract them from material sensations. Plato believed that the lions (the Forms) were already in their zoo cages (the mind's concepts), while Aristotle believed that they had to be found in the jungle (the material world) and then brought home (abstracted) from there and put into the cage of the mind's concepts.

In his ethics Aristotle believes in objective and universal goods (a "natural moral law") just as Plato does, but he believes that the form or essence of each moral virtue is a mean between two extremes regarding the virtue's matter or material content. This content consists in passions (emotions, feelings) and physical actions. E.g., courage is feeling neither too little nor too much fear, and being neither foolhardy nor over-cautious in actions. In each virtue, reason imposes the right form onto material actions and irrational passions, somewhat as a cookie cutter imposes form on cookie dough.

Aristotle also denied Plato's political idea that there was one most perfect form of government, and held instead that rule by one, by some, or by all, could be either good or bad depending on whether the rulers ruled for their people or for themselves, whether the rule was of law or of will, and whether the people were not just subjectively satisfied but truly happy (blessed) as a result.

2. Epicurus: Hedonism (Roman, 3nd century B.C.)

Like the Sophists rather than Plato, Epicureans are usually atheists and materialists. Since they do not recognize the existence of gods, immortal souls, or spiritual realities, their concept of the greatest good is simply pleasure, though intelligently regulated by reason so that it does not become self-destructive. ("Hedonism" comes from the Greek word for pleasure, *hedone.*) When the world goes mad and sad, one can still achieve happiness (pleasure) by carefully cultivating one's own garden of delights, especially food and sex.

3. Pyrrho: Skepticism (2rd century B.C.)

Skepticism denies the top two quarters of Plato's "divided line" in book 6 of the *Republic,* i.e., it denies the possibility of any certain knowledge of truth. Skepticism, in the late classical world, was a practical philosophy for saving one's sanity and peace of mind in a world in crisis. If truth is unattainable, we don't have to be frustrated by trying to attain it. (Stoicism, Epicureanism, and Neoplatonism are alternative means to the same peace-of-mind goal.) But it doesn't really end unhappiness, it just ends hope. Minds need truth as eyes need light.

4. Epictetus: Stoicism (Roman, 2nd century B.C.)

Stoicism was the most popular school of philosophy in the Hellenistic era (the Greek world after

Alexander the Great) and throughout most of the history of Rome. There were many famous Stoic philosophers, such as Seneca the senator and Marcus Aurelius the emperor, but Epictetus, who was a slave, wrote its shortest and handiest handbook, the *Enchiridion.*

Stoicism differs from Plato in two important ways. First, it is not a metaphysic. It is practical rather than theoretical. It is addressed to the problem of attaining virtue, wisdom, and happiness in a corrupt, foolish, and miserable world. Second, its main means to this end is to sharply distinguish what is in our power and what is not, and to confine all desires and actions to the few things that are in our power, especially the acts of our reason and will rather than our emotions or what happens in the world outside us. Stoicism sees emotions as the main source of misery and counsels the total control, or even suppression, of emotion by reason. Plato, in contrast, taught the *education* of emotions and desires, beginning with the first such educational step, music.

5. Plotinus: Mysticism (Roman-Egyptian, 3rd century A.D.)

Plotinus, founder of Neo-Platonism, identified Plato's "Idea of the Good" with "The One," which he conceived as infinite and mystically transcending all reason. Reason could not know the infinite One (1) because reason always involved the duality of knower and known, or subject and object, and also (2) because reason required finitude in its object, whether that object was physical (things like dog vs. cat) or spiritual (Ideas like justice vs. injustice).

6. St. Augustine: Christian Platonism (Roman-African, 4th century A.D.)

In the *Confessions* Augustine credits Plato with freeing him from materialistic thinking and introducing him to eternal truths, especially the Idea of the Absolute Good, but faults Plato for not giving him a personal relationship to this eternal truth, which Plato identified as an Idea but which Christianity identifies as a Person.

Philosophically, Augustine completed Plato by giving his Ideas a home in the Mind of God.

7. St. Thomas Aquinas: Christian Aristotelianism (Italian, 13th century)

Aquinas combines Aristotle's and Augustine's corrections to Plato. The Ideas, he says, do not exist in themselves, as Plato thought, but only in the Mind of God, as Augustine says; and they exist as the forms of material things, as Aristotle said, and as concepts in our mind, which abstracts them from things.

Almost all medieval philosophers tried in some way to synthesize Plato with Aristotle, as well as with Christianity.

8. Machiavelli: "Machiavellianism" (Italian, 15th century)

The contrasts are almost total. Machiavelli blames classical authors like Plato for teaching us how to be good; he says we need to learn how to be evil, in order to be successful. It is the philosophy of Gyges: injustice, if clever enough, is more profitable than justice.

Thus Machiavelli's presuppositions are pragmatism rather than idealism (thus the end of practical success justifies any means that works to get it), materialism rather than spiritualism (thus all men are in competition, like pieces of matter, and therefore not to be trusted), and relativism rather than moralism (thus promises are to be kept only when it is to your own advantage).

9. Bacon: The Conquest of Nature by Technology (English, 16th century)

For Plato and all the classical pre-modern thinkers, knowledge is first of all for truth. Truth is the absolute. Bacon criticizes this: knowledge of truth is important, but not for its own sake: it is for power, for "man's conquest of nature" by applied science (technology). This is as radical a change as there can be: it is a new *summum bonum*, a new answer to the question: What is the supreme good?

To that end, Bacon prefers physical sensation over spiritual wisdom and inductive reason, which is based on physical sensation, over deductive reasoning, which is based on abstract general principles.

10. Descartes: Philosophy by Scientific Method (French, 17th century)

Descartes narrows the broad thing Plato meant by "reason" to mathematical, scientific-method reasoning. He wants to de-capitalize Plato's Reason. He wants to make philosophy a mathematical kind of science, a quasi-geometrical system of deductions. In other words, his goal is the third quarter of Plato's "divided line" rather than the fourth. He does this in order to bring to philosophy the same kind of progress and universal agreement that the scientific method was bringing to all the other sciences: the resolving of all problems and the ending of all disputes. Descartes thought that these disputes were the philosophical bases of the religious and political ideologies that were the source of most serious wars, especially the terrible and traumatizing Thirty Years' War that Descartes lived through.

Descartes sets out to be the new Socrates, starting philosophy off afresh with a radically new method, ignoring all his predecessors. Yet he repeats (and exaggerates) many typically Platonic themes, especially the existence of eternal truths (Platonic Forms); the rule of reason, the existence, spirituality and immortality of the soul; the tracing of all evil back to ignorance; a two-substance anthropology (body and soul are "clear and distinct"); and a rationalistic ("innate ideas") rather than empiricist epistemology.

11. Spinoza: Pantheism (Dutch-Portuguese, 17th century)

Spinoza uses Descartes's new mathematical-scientific method in philosophy to a different end.

For Spinoza there are not two levels of reality, as there are for Plato and Descartes. God and nature are a single substance, looked at from two different angles. Materialists deny the Creator; pantheists deny the creation. Plato does not teach the notion of creation (it is a distinctively Jewish idea), but he has the same two worlds of the eternal (the Ideas) and the temporal (things).

12. Hobbes: Materialism (English, 17th century)

Nothing exists except matter, for Hobbes. Thus God and the soul are "subtle" bodies; Heaven is political stability on earth, and reason is only the slave of the senses. Because man, like all matter, is essentially selfish and competitive, and because the natural state of man is "nasty, solitary, poor, brutish, and short," only an absolute monarchy, which Hobbes called a "Leviathan" (great beast) and which Plato called a tyranny, can force man to act justly, contrary to his nature.

13. Pascal: Faith as a Wager (French, 17th century)

Pascal is really the first "existentialist." He despairs of understanding the mysteries of human existence, such as injustice and death, by abstract reason. Only concrete, personal religious faith, embraced by a "wager" (later existentialists will call it a "leap") can deliver the hope of true, deep, and lasting happiness. The only true answer to the four greatest questions in the world—who God is, who man is, what the meaning of life is, and what the meaning of death is—is Jesus Christ, embraced by faith and love, not by the new scientific meaning of reason. In this world reason is weaker than imagination, justice is weaker than injustice, death always wins over life, and uncertainty refutes certainty. Love (charity) is as transcendent of reason as reason is transcendent of matter. "The heart (love—which, by the way, is not feeling or sentiment, as it is for Rousseau) has its reasons which the reason does not know."

14. Rousseau: "Romanticism" (French, 18th century)

Rousseau is as skeptical of reason as Pascal is, but his substitute is not religious faith in divine revelation but human feeling and emotion. Evil comes not from ignorance, and not from within human nature (which is innocent) but from the alienating structures of society, beginning with private property. Where Hobbes taught that man is by nature evil and selfish and only a strong society (an absolute monarchy, the "Leviathan") could force him to act justly, out of fear, contrary to his nature, Rousseau taught the opposite: that man is by nature good and innocent, and that the villain, rather than the hero, is artificial society which induces him to live contrary to his nature and instinctive feelings, especially pity and compassion. Both Hobbes and Rousseau demean reason, mainly because they no longer accept (or perhaps even understand) Plato's broad meaning of the term, but only Descartes's narrowed, mathematical meaning.

15. Locke: Empiricism (English, 18th century)

Plato, like Descartes, is a Rationalist. Reason has a direct access to truth. But for Empiricists, this is not so since there are no innate ideas and reason is dependent on sense experience. In fact reason is only the arrangement of sensations. Abstract reason is not to be trusted, but must be judged by sense experience.

Aristotle is a "soft" Empiricist: he agrees that all knowledge begins with sense experience but not that it ends with it. Reason, for Aristotle, can abstract universal forms (incarnate Platonic Ideas) from matter. Empiricists deny this. They are Nominalists, i.e., they reduce universals (what Plato called Ideas and Aristotle forms) to names ("nomina") rather than objective realities.

16. Berkeley: Immaterialism (Irish, 18th century)

Hobbes denied the existence of anything other than matter, but Berkeley denied the existence of matter! He is an "idealist" in the sense that he believes that there is nothing except ideas and the minds (divine or human) that perceive them. His "big idea" is that *esse est percipi*, "to be is to be perceived (known)." What we call matter is only God's ideas. The material world keeps existing even when we stop perceiving it only because God keeps perceiving it.

Plato is a dualist: immaterial, eternal Ideas AND material things. Hobbes denies the first half of the dualism (the world outside the Cave); Berkeley denies the second half (the Cave).

17. Hume: Skepticism (Scotch, 18th century)

Hume took Locke's Empiricist principles and deduced the logical consequence of skepticism from them. We have no certain knowledge except empty, factually non-informative logical tautologies like X=X, which he calls "relations of ideas." The only other knowledge we have is sensory "matters of fact," which are always contingent and only probable, never certain. We do not even know with certainty that the sun will rise tomorrow or that birds lay eggs. To have seen it in the past does not prove that we will see it in the future. Knowledge of reality is limited to sense experience, and sense experience delivers only "this happened," never "this necessarily happens." There are no Platonic Ideas OR Aristotelian forms. Hume is a radical Nominalist, as far from Plato's Ideas as possible.

18. Kant: Epistemological Idealism (German, 18th century)

Kant tried to mediate the dispute between what he called "dogmatism and skepticism," i.e., between the Cartesian rationalists, with their certainties deduced from "innate ideas," and the skeptical Humean Empiricists, by teaching that reason and the senses work together, as Aristotle said, but not by Aristotle's way of abstracting universal and necessary forms from particular, contingent material things, but rather by imposing on the unformed and unknowable world of our experience these innate mental forms or categories (such as time and space in physics, categories like causality and possibility in logic, and ideas like God and immortality in metaphysics). In other words, what we think is science (discovery) is really art (construction, creation). This is his "big idea," which he called "the Copernican Revolution in philosophy." It is really a redefinition of truth as the conformity of its object to the knowing mind rather than of the knowing mind to its object. For Kant, Platonic Ideas exist, but only subjectively, in our minds. However, all minds must work in the same way: the Ideas are necessary and universal. These Ideas are not really Platonic Ideas with a capital I but only Ideas with a small i: our minds do not discover them but create them.

19. Hegel: Historical Relativism (German, 19th century)

Hegel, unlike Kant, believes Platonic Ideas exist objectively and can be known. However, they are not eternal, but change. All is change. Truth itself changes in history. History is the growth of God, or "the Absolute." Everything is a stage in this evolution. Hegel is a pantheist, like Spinoza, but also, unlike Spinoza, a historical relativist. Plato is neither.

20. Marx: Communism (German, 19th century)

Marxism, or Communism, is called "dialectical materialism" because it accepts Hegel's claim that everything evolves through history (historical relativism) through a dialectical process, as Hegel said, of a conflict between two forces, the "thesis" and the "antithesis," which are reconciled into a "higher synthesis"; but the content of this historical process, for Marx, is material, not spiritual, as it was for Hegel. It is not an evolution of God (Marx is an atheist) but of matter (he is a materialist).

Politically, Marx taught the communal, collective ownership of all the means of production (of wealth) for everyone (thus there is to be no private property, nor even private families). Plato restricted this to the small class of the "guardians" or philosopher-kings, like Catholic monks. Marxism abolishes classes and substitutes absolute equality, a "classless society."

Marx also taught that this Utopian "classless society" could come about not through rational persuasion, which was Plato's method, but only by violent revolution.

21. Mill: Utilitarianism (English, 19th century)

Utilitarianism is an ethical philosophy that claims that good is simply happiness, happiness is simply pleasure, and pleasure is subjective, so there is no objective, universal moral absolute like Plato's "Idea of the Good." Utilitarianism is skeptical of metaphysics, of teleology (real objective purposes or natural ends) and of any natural moral law. The only universal rule is to do whatever you think will produce "the greatest happiness for the greatest number," i.e., to maximize pleasure by both quality and quantity: whatever makes the most people the most happy is good. This end justifies any means. Neither justice nor duty nor God nor any "natural law" judges this. The virtue Plato wrote the whole *Republic* about, Justice, does not judge actions.

Nietzsche called this "the pig philosophy." But Mill said that "it is better to be Socrates dissatisfied than a pig satisfied." His "happiness," though subjective, is not just satisfaction or contentment.

22. Kierkegaard: Christian Existentialism (Danish, 19th century)

Like Pascal, and unlike Plato, Kierkegaard emphasized faith over reason, the subjective over the objective, the concrete individual person over the abstract impersonal universal, and the supernatural (divine grace) over the natural (human efforts).

Kierkegaard thought Socrates was the greatest of philosophers, but saw him as limited to "the ethical stage" of human existence as distinct from "the religious stage." (The four main differences between these two "stages on life's way" are in the first paragraph.) Both Socrates and Jesus, both ethics and religion transcend the "aesthetic stage," whose ultimate good is neither objective reason nor personal faith but pleasure and power (Bacon, Machiavelli, Hobbes, Marx, and Mill).

23. Nietzsche: Atheistic Existentialism (German, 19th century)

Nietzsche is the total anti-Platonist. Nietzsche, like Kierkegaard, focuses on Socrates and Christ as the two foci of all of philosophy and human history. But while they are Kierkegaard's two heroes, they are Nietzsche's two villains. He calls himself the "Anti-Christ." He is also the anti-Socrates and the anti-Plato. Nietzsche's most famous saying, "God is dead," means that what died in the hearts of individuals and of Western civilization in the modern age was not only the God of Christianity but also the God of Platonism: the transcendent realm of Ideas; objective truth, goodness, and beauty; philosophy, morality, and religion; everything outside the Cave.

Nietzsche called himself "the philosopher with a hammer," the hammer of suspicion and cynicism which smashed into smithereens, as if they were fragile glass, not only God but also gods, such as "the will to truth," free will, the dignity or intrinsic value of man, the soul, immortality, and objectively binding morality, especially the Christian morality of love. For Nietzsche, there are not "more things in heaven and earth (i.e., in reality) than in your philosophies," as Hamlet said to Horatio, but fewer.

One who thus kills both God and His image in himself (the will to conform to objective truth and the will to goodness, i.e., conscience) transcends humanity and becomes a "super-man." (For a profound exploration of this "new man" read Dostoyevski's *Crime and Punishment.)*

24. Heidegger: Ontological (Being-directed) Existentialism (German, 20th century)

Heidegger blames Plato above all other philosophers for what he calls "the forgetfulness of Being" which (he says) characterizes all of subsequent Western philosophy. It is difficult to understand what Heidegger means by Being, but it is clear that he does not mean the objects of reason, essences, or Platonic Ideas. He says that error was connected with the error of reducing Truth to a correspondence between reason and its objects.

Heidegger says the best path to understand Being is to begin not with the beings of nature but with human being, human existence. He calls this "Dasein," or "being-there," or "being-in-the-world," and he sees this as fundamentally different than, and not an example of, beings or substances or entities, or objects of reason, since being-in-the-world is subjective, or subjectivity rather than objective. Being itself is neither the being of an object or essence nor the being of a subject or thinker, but the common field in which both appear and distinguish themselves from each other.

And that's just about the easiest possible way to simplify Heidegger!

25. Sartre: Nihilistic existentialism (French, 20th century)

Begin with Heidegger's dualism or radical distinction between the being of objects and the being of subjects, then drop Being itself, and you get Sartre. For him there is no Being; he is a "nihilist." (That is what "nihilism" means.) There are only "being-in-itself" (objects) and "being-for-itself" (human subjects) but no "being."

Being would function like God, as the absolute. But Sartre calls his philosophy "an attempt to draw out all the consequences of atheism." He does this in a more cerebral and logical way than Nietzsche, but with essentially the same conclusions, especially in the sphere of human relationships, where Platonic Justice does not exist and all that is left is a Nietzschean "will to power" over others. Each human subject (or "being-for-itself") seeks to reduce each other to an object (a "being-in-itself").

Not only is Justice impossible, but also unselfish love, either of other people (who exist) or of Platonic Ideas such as real truth, goodness, or beauty (which do not exist, according to Sartre).

26. Husserl: Phenomenology (Austrian, 20th century)

Husserl founded a new philosophical method, which he called "phenomenology" because it confines itself to describing the "phenomena," or immediate appearance of things, and confines thinking to thinking which has stripped itself of all presuppositions. It is a sort of inner empiricism that seeks to carefully tabulate how all things appear in human consciousness, without judging whether they are objective realities or not. In this way Husserl attempted to discover essences (Platonic Forms) as objects of consciousness by beginning with consciousness itself. Use of this method (phenomenology is not a doctrine, but a method) demands very slow, patient inner observation rather than the quick, dramatic strokes of Socratic syllogistic arguments. It wants not to prove, just to see.

27. James: Pragmatism (American, 20th century)

William James, founder and namer of America's only indigenous philosophy, "pragmatism," defined it as a method of testing ideas by looking at their practical results in experience rather than at their logical presuppositions or premises. It does not either affirm or deny Platonism, but looks in the opposite direction: ideas are judged meaningful, and thus either true or false, if and only if we can specify how they *make a difference* in our lives. (By this standard, most of Plato's ideas are very meaningful indeed; in fact the *Republic* may be regarded as an extended answer to that very question concerning Justice.)

28. Dewey: Ideological Pragmatism (American, 20th century)

John Dewey, the most influential educational philosopher of modern times and the founder of "progressive education," took pragmatism in a social, political, and ideological direction, allying it with liberal or left-wing political and educational programs and scorning traditional ones, especially regarding transcendent religion, metaphysical philosophy, and ethical absolutes. Though his pragmatic method is the same as that of James, his conclusions (or rather presuppositions) are the opposite: atheism, scientific rationalism, materialism, and determinism. (James defended "the will to believe," spirituality, religious mysticism, and free will.) Dewey is to James, among the pragmatists, what the Sophists were to Socrates among the Greeks.

29. Moore: Ordinary Language (English, 20th century)

G. E. Moore founded the "ordinary language analysis" version of "analytic philosophy," which focuses on the logic of language and the meaning of words in a way that reminds us of Socrates' dialogs but in a much more slow and excruciatingly careful and exacting way. Moore contrasts sharply with other "analytic philosophers" such as A. J. Ayer, Bertrand Russell, and the early Wittgenstein, who used mathematical logic to invent an artificial language to solve (or rather dissolve) all traditional philosophical problems.

30. Wittgenstein: Linguistic Analysis (Austrian, 20th century)

The early Wittgenstein, in his *Tractatus Logico-Philosophicus,* reduced all meaning to "atomic propositions" which copied or pictured empirical facts. Everything that most people find importantly meaningful, especially ethics, was simply unsayable by this newly constricted language system. Its last sentence was its most important: "Whereof one cannot speak, thereof he must be silent." This Wittgenstein called "the mystical," and included ethics, religion, and aesthetics. He later repudiated this philosophy in his posthumously published *Philosophical Investigations,* and explored the many flexible and relative uses of "language games," including non-literal terms; but he never ventured directly into metaphysics or ethics, as Plato did.

31. Derrida: Deconstructionism (French, 20th century)

No one ever more directly confronted and repudiated Plato's fundamental logical assumption than Derrida. His central idea, "differance" (a coy

French way to say "difference"), is an attack on what he calls "purity," by which he meant the identity or intelligible consistency of literally anything (except Deconstructionism itself). There are no Platonic Ideas or essences or identities. Everything is *not what it is.* Derrida applies this to everything he touches. Everything is "deconstructed," nothing stays, everything becomes subject to indefensible "interpretations." There is no "world" outside of and distinct from any literary "text." It is an attack on the very existence of objective truth.

I take seriously and learn something from every philosophical school in history—except this one. I cannot and do not believe Deconstructionists are both sane and serious. Since they are sane enough to acquire prestigious philosophical positions, I can only conclude that they are not serious, but laughing up their sleeves at us who take them seriously, as they jerk our chains and play sneering little games with us. Arguing with them is fruitless. It also grants them much too much respect by taking them at their word. Play their own game of "*differance*" with them. When they attack the essence of Platonism, call them Platonists. And be grateful to them for helping us to appreciate Plato by contrast, as death helps us appreciate life.

Postscript

Where do we go from here? If you, as a beginner, have made a beginning, what comes after the beginning?

For more on Plato, read all his dialogs.

For good secondary sources on Plato, read A. E. Taylor, Paul Shorey, or Paul Elmer More.

For a political interpretation of the *Republic,* read Allan Bloom.

For another introduction to philosophy via Plato's *Apology of Socrates,* read *Philosophy 101 by Socrates,* by the author.

For an exploration of the historical importance of Plato in Western intellectual history, read *The Platonic Tradition* by the author.

For examples of Socrates dialoging with later philosophers (Machiavelli, Sartre, Marx, Descartes, Hume, Kant, Kierkegaard, and Freud), read these eight books beginning with the words *Socrates Meets* by the author.

For an introduction to the 100 greatest philosophers of all time, read SOCRATES' CHILDREN, in four volumes, by the author.

For an introduction to traditional common-sense, ordinary-language logic (not modern mathematical logic, or symbolic logic), see *Socratic Logic,* by the author.

For applications to your own life, write some Socratic dialogs yourself (it's surprisingly easy and fun!) about issues that matter to you in your world and your life. It's great cognitive therapy.

You have begun the serious study of philosophy, one of the greatest enterprises in the history of civilization. I wish you a good journey, which will never end.